Three Gates to Hell

by Jim Tucker
with Virginia Koehler and Don Tanner

Gift Publications
Costa Mesa, California 92626

Bible references are taken from the King James Version.

Three Gates to Hell

Copyright © 1980 by Gift Publications

Published by Gift Publications
Costa Mesa, California 92626

Library of Congress Catalog Card Number 80-67299
ISBN 0-86595-001-6

All rights reserved. No portion of this book may be reproduced in any form without the written permission of the publisher.

Printed in the United States of America

Contents

Acknowledgments

With the exception of a few, the names of people mentioned in this book have been changed to protect the privacy of the individual and/or their families.

FOREWORD

"I would hate God if I did not know Him personally. I would hate Him for letting so much hurt happen to a little boy," said one reviewer of this manuscript.

Considering Jim Tucker's horrible childhood, one cannot possibly explain the man apart from God. The brutalization of the lad and confinement for twenty-seven years infected him with a hate to match his huge physique.

Isolated for three years in a solitary confinement cell, empty of any furnishings—even a bed—and with only a hole in the floor for a toilet, Big Jim insulated himself against the risk of further hurt.

Christ used one man, an ex-con named Phil Thatcher, to penetrate Jim's armor. Later, when Demos Shakarian, founder and president of the Full Gospel Business Men's Fellowship, Enoch Christofferson, then mayor of Turlock, and others opened their hearts to him, doors of ministry were also opened.

Jim's New Life Crusade is to duplicate and multiply the kindness Phil Thatcher showed him. He meets men at the prison gate, takes them into his home, provides food and shelter, offers spiritual counseling and assists them in obtaining employment. Out of the two hundred forty-two men whom he has taken out of prison in the last eighteen months, only nine have returned.

Jim's prayer, and mine, is that *Three Gates to Hell* will be used to reach thousands of prisoners with the message of love and hope that has so dramatically changed his life.

Nelson B. Melvin, D.D.
Senior Editor
Voice Magazine

Chapter 1
IN THE "HOLE"

Trying to look older than my seventeen years, I ambled into the dark bar more from boredom than desire for a drink. The bright sunlight had felt good after the damp chill of a night spent sleeping in a doorway. But now the good feeling was beginning to wear thin.

I can't be coming down already! I frowned. *Man, I've got to put some cash together. My stash is gettin' low . . .*

"Hi, lover!" A girl at the bar interrupted my thoughts and motioned me to the empty stool beside her.

She wasn't especially attractive; no girl had been since Jane, but this one soon let me know that she was down on her luck, too. She knew of a dairy that we could rob together. Although preferring to work alone, I went with her to look it over. The dairy was a huge plant, including a retail store where ice cream was sold. I sprang for a cone and, as we sat casing the place, decided it would be a cinch.

"Gotta plan?" Julia asked.

"If you can get a car, and drive, I'll go in tonight after hours. I'll take the money from the register and, if I can find the safe fast, I'll crack it; otherwise, we'd better get out quick."

Julia got the car and, in the wee hours of the morning,

dropped me off on the black streets. I jimmied a window to the dairy with no trouble, but was hardly inside before hearing the muffled tread of the watchman's footsteps. Sprinting through the plant, I gave up looking for the safe and headed for the register in the store. Stealthily, I slid out of my shoes to walk without a sound. I opened the register and swore; only a few dollars there. Not nearly enough! I just couldn't skip with this measly amount of dough. Split two ways, it wouldn't even get us through a good day. Maybe the safe was in the back of the store.

I crept around refrigerator bins of popsicles and Neapolitan ice-cream sandwiches, finally finding the safe in an obscure corner of a storeroom.

Suddenly the scream of sirens—closer and closer! Some way the cops must have been tipped off. I leaped back toward the register for the money and my shoes, but before I reached the counter the white beams of a flashlight blinded me.

"Security guard!" A stern voice behind the light shouted.

I dashed to the back of the building, leaving all behind, opened a door and scrambled over a high fence, thanks to old metal oil drums stacked beside it.

How lucky can you get! I panted. *If Julia's circling the block until I hit the corner, like we planned, we'll have it made—never mind the money or my shoes.* My foot was cut on some barbed wire on the fence, but that would be a small price to pay for getting away.

The black car was there, right at the corner. I opened the driver's side front door before realizing it was an unmarked patrol car.

"Freeze!" yelled a plainclothes officer behind the wheel, and the barrel of a shotgun poked toward my chest. Another cop in the front seat smirked:

"You in a hurry to get somewhere—or do you just want good company?"

"Excuse me. I thought you were my girl."

"Oh, she pickin' you up about now?"

"Well, maybe—you know."

"No, tell us about it. Where have you been barefooted to cut your foot like that?"

"Oh, I uh—just around, you know."

"No, I told you, we don't know. Who is your girl?"

"Just a girl. I'll get out of your hair now."

"You'd better stay a little longer," the cop behind the wheel said. "We got another stop to make right here."

They had me. I knew it. They knew it. One stayed with me in the car, and the other checked with the watchman. They brought out my shoes and the money I'd left behind.

"Looks like you could use these shoes, if they don't hurt your feet. Here, try 'em on."

Reluctantly, I slipped them on.

"Now, let's go get that girl who stood you up. Where'd you last see her?"

"I don't know," I lied. They found her anyway, hanging around the bar down the street. She was sleeping—or pretended to be—at one of the tables, but she got the picture real fast.

"Sorry I wasn't able to keep our date, but I had something to take care of with the police," I grinned sheepishly, taking the rap.

Since nothing was actually stolen, I got off light by copping a plea of breaking and entering and attempted theft. Even so, I was sentenced to three months in the local jail for violating parole. That was easy time. At least I got fed and had a place to sleep. But it was still the lockup.

What a screw-up! I cursed my stupidity while lying on my bunk. *How many times you been in here, man—and not all of them this easy, either. Don't you ever learn? How long is it gonna take you to quit getting caught, anyhow? Lousy breaks—that's all I've had all my life. Well, maybe I've had one good break,* I smirked cynically. I couldn't be tried as an adult yet. So I had awhile to get even with everyone before being sent up for life.

Someone said we make our own breaks. I didn't believe it for a minute. What could I have done about my dad splitting the minute I was born? Still, things weren't *that* bad, until that night when I was seven. Talk about a lousy break! And I don't see what I could have done about that, either. I shut my mind off. Tried, at least. Dredging up the past was stupid. The anger and hatred surged in me even more when I thought about my splintered existence.

But, man, thinking was all there was to do in the hole. I looked around my cell and sneered, *You've seen one, you've seen 'em all.*

As I lay on the hard cot, my mind grudgingly wandered into the past when I was only seven.

"I can count, Mama! Should I count the cars for you?"

"Yes, Jimmy."

"One. Two. Three. Are you listening, Mama?"

"I'm tired, Jimmy. Keep hold of Jackie's hand. Don't let him fall when we get off the trolley."

"I've got him. Are you sick again, Mama?"

"I'll be all right when I get to bed."

"I'll help Jackie climb the stairs, Mama. It was fun walking at Central Market. I like it when we walk together, Mama."

A clear picture of my beautiful, young mother was still in my mind.

"Put the meat in the icebox, Jimmy, while I put Jackie in the crib. Then get ready for bed."

"But I'm thirsty, Mama, and hungry."

"All right, use a chair and get a drink of water, but don't touch the butcher knives on the drainboard. Now, be a good boy and move the irons over on the stove. In a minute I'll warm something for you."

"You'd better take your pills, Mama, and I can put some stew in the pan. Look, I'm your helper, huh Mama? I'm strong! I can even lift Jackie!"

"You're a good boy, Jimmy. And my helper! Now, eat so we can get to bed. I'm very tired."

"Don't go to sleep yet, Mama. Talk to me while I eat, and you can rest. Are you better now? Does the medicine in the bottle help, too? You need lots of pills and medicine, Mama, and when I grow up I'll work for you, Mama, so you can get well."

"Be quiet now, Jimmy, and don't wake Jackie. He's not as big and strong as you."

"If I'm good, can I lie down beside you, Mama?"

It was good to have Mama all to myself, to see her beautiful red hair fall about her shoulders as I snuggled next to her.

"Mama, why did the men at Central Market say you looked like my sister? Even some people on the trolley said that one day! Remember, Mama?"

"Be quiet, Jim, I wanna sleep."

"Don't go to sleep yet. Please. Sing to me about *The Man*. Then, when you're sleeping I'll climb up and sleep by Jackie and watch him for you."

Mother agreed but reminded me to first latch the screen and bolt the door. I really loved the song about the garden and *The*

Man who walked and talked with Mama! She could sing—my young mom from Oklahoma! Her soft voice made the song a lullaby.

And He walks with me, and He talks with me,
And He tells me I am His own,
And the joys we share, as we tarry there,
None other has ever known!

Once I'd asked her, "Is *The Man* in the garden my daddy?"

"No, Jimmy, just a man, I guess. I learned the song back home. There was a garden there, too."

When Mama was asleep, I checked the bolt and latch on the door, then climbed into the crib that I shared with my brother. Mama had always told me to be sure they were locked—because of the stairs. I had to see to it that Jackie didn't get out into the hall while she was sleeping.

I thought about our trolley ride and walk at Central Market that day. It was fun for us three. The street light came into the narrow window of our apartment that was really just one big room. The linoleum on the kitchen floor was clean, and the old, bright rug under Mama's bed, the old, wooden dresser and our crib had been swept clean with a broom that day.

It had been Mama's day off from work. While she did housework and ironing, Jackie and I roughhoused in the hall, keeping careful on the stairs. Jackie was a real pal, and I liked being his older brother. I was only a year older, so it must have been my larger size that made him and Mama feel that I was able to look after him. That night, in the crib beside Jackie, I felt good—like I belonged somewhere—and was happy.

Then I began to wonder. Would Mama ever get well? Would Daddy ever come back? Would I ever meet *The Man* Mama had walked with? From the way she sang, I wanted to know Him. I glanced at my sleeping mother, then at Jackie, and dreamed of a time when I'd grow up and really take care of both of them.

My eyes drifted to the kitchen area. I saw the butcher knives that I was told never to touch and the old, two-piece flatirons on the stove. A couple of magazines stacked neatly on the table reminded me of the times when Mama let us sit on each side of her while we looked at the pictures together.

The song about the garden and *The Man* came back to my mind. If I could just get us a daddy like *The Man*—except he would stay with us and not just sometimes walk with people in a garden! A good man like that would keep us together more, and Mama could stop working and not get so tired. And she'd get well and not need all those pills and medicines from the bottles.

I got kind of tired and snuggled close to Jackie when I heard a loud noise at the door. Jackie woke up, and we both yelled "Mama! Mama!"

Somebody was ripping the screen door off! Then came a racket like the old, wooden door being smashed in. I yelled for Mama, but she heard nothing. Then the door broke open, and a giant shadow ran into the room, picked up the knives and irons and, as we screamed, began to hit our mother over and over again with all his might. We yelled for him to stop but he kept on and shouted, "Shut up or I'll cut *your* heads off!"

Chapter 2
"SOMEDAY I'LL GET EVEN"

We shut up. He meant what he said! Frightened, we buried our heads under the blanket, afraid to breathe.

Suddenly someone far away yelled, and we could hear hurrying footsteps coming toward our apartment. The man ran out and down the steep flight of stairs. Jackie and I started to breathe again. He had been scared off. Now we wouldn't get hurt! But—what about Mama?

I threw back the blanket and looked. It was kind of dark, but what I saw made me sick. Mama's face was crushed, and her long, beautiful, red hair was soaked in blood all over the pillow.

The light in our apartment suddenly clicked on, and people in the doorway gasped. Voices yelled, "Call an ambulance! Call the police! There are kids in here."

I'd never seen so many people in one place. They would peek in and then run out. When the police came, the ambulance attendants first took Mama from the bed. "Oh, no!" one of them said, as they carefully loaded her onto a stretcher.

"I wanna go with Mama!" I yelled. Even though I felt sick to my stomach, I climbed out of the crib. Jackie screamed, and then a calm voice said, "Take it easy! We need you here. Maybe we can find the person who did this. Now, don't you want to be a big boy and help us?"

I looked up into the kind face of a police officer and nodded.

"Good!" he smiled. "What's your name—and your brother's?"

"Jimmy Tucker. He's Jackie."

"Do you know who did this, Jimmy? Was it your dad?"

"No—but it wasn't Daddy."

"Where *is* Daddy?"

"He left us. "

"Will he be back?"

"No. "

"Why not? Jimmy, how do you know he won't be back?"

"Mama said."

"When did you last see your father?"

"I don't know. He never comes here no more."

More questions followed. Things I don't remember any more, except that I was glad when Officer James said we were done. "Okay, Jimmy, now you and your brother go with these people, and I'll see you later. They'll take good care of you, okay?"

Riding in a car instead of a trolley, we were taken to a building called Los Angeles Juvenile Hall. They gave us a bath, dressed us in pajamas and put us to bed. All the while I kept asking, "Where is Mama?" and the same answer was repeated, "In the hospital."

Jackie couldn't stop crying and woke up the other kids, so they took him somewhere else to sleep. I missed him right away. For the first time, we didn't sleep together. In that big room in the small, strange bed, I was scared.

Everything that had taken place in the apartment kept coming into my mind over and over. Why had it happened? Oh, if I had only been grown up! I would have kept that man away from Mama.

Mama! Mama! Where are you, Mama? Are you really dead in the hospital? No one told me that the dead weren't kept in the hospital.

I wondered about Jackie. He should be with me! Mama had told me to always look after him. Well, maybe tomorrow things would be different. Maybe someone would listen to me. I'd be very grown-up and *make* them understand!

The next day they let us go into the playground for a while, and I saw Jackie there. He was still crying, but not so loud. He was staying in a room with a bunch of girls and wanted to be with me. I told him *I'd* fix it.

As confidently as a seven-year-old can, I marched into a room and asked who was in charge. Someone laughed and waved me into an office.

"I'm *always* in charge of Jackie when Mama isn't around, so you'd better let him be with me until we go!" I demanded of the person there.

But I was soon put in my place. Jackie would do as he was told and so would I, *or* there were ways of seeing to it that we did! Having to admit to Jackie that I couldn't work it out made me mad. "Someday I'll get even!" I told myself. "Just you wait . . . all of you!"

Except for Jackie, I seldom spoke to anyone during my remaining time at Juvenile Hall. Grief, worry, and trying to get used to the place were too much for me. Because I saw how the boys in my dorm were, I walked around trying to look tough, hoping to avoid a fight. They were older and knew a lot of tricks I had never seen before. Like the day I was in the shower room and some of the older boys began to tease me.

"Hey, kid! You're not very friendly!"

"Yeah, think yer bettr'n us, or somethin'?"

"Well, kid . . . ya wanna be friendly or not?"

I knew it was either be friendly or fight. "S . . . sure," I stammered, glancing from one guy to the other.

"Let's shower together then!"

"Okay." I didn't know what they would do next. Quickly two boys shoved me struggling against a wall. They held me in place, threw a towel over my head, and put some greasy stuff into my behind.

They took turns. It hurt, and I was ashamed. When they finished, the roughest member of the gang yelled a warning in my ear. "You tell, and you'll be in big trouble. Don't and you can be one of us. It's up to you, kid."

I was mad and knew better than to fight. I ran to my bed, pulled the covers over my head and cried. It hurt so much in back. Nothing in my life bothered me more. If only I could be with Mama. I fell asleep wishing that *The Man* in the garden would come and fight for me, and be my dad.

Shortly afterward, Jackie and I were called into the office of the superintendent and told to get ready to leave. A nice home had been found where we could be together. Did that make us happy?

We nodded our heads, and I put my arm around Jackie as he grinned up at me. "See, Jim, *you did it*!

Chapter 3
COMPANIONS TO A PATSY

The big car didn't impress me. It was more fun riding with Mama on the trolley. Why didn't the voice saying how youngsters like us needed a "nice Mrs. Ames and her staff" just shut up? I was in no mood to "get ready to be introduced," as the social worker put it.

Angry thoughts poured over my mind. *For sure now, the lousy b— killed her! Mama's dead in the hospital or else she'd be taking us back home, and we wouldn't be riding in this car!* I didn't know what the word meant. I'd learned it since coming to "juvy," and it seemed to mean something terrible. And that's how I felt. *That's what you are, you killer! A b—! And a lousy one, too!"*

A few words from the voice about "our situation" and how "You boys will be very happy here, providing you obey the rules and don't make trouble," got through to me. Then I tuned it out.

What I'd like to do to you, you lousy b— rat, is a-plenty! Mama looked so young and pretty that people at Central Market even thought she was my sister! Just you wait, you lousy . . . .

Jackie's voice caught my attention. "We're here, Jimmy! Look, a yard and grass!"

"Yeah?"

"Maybe we *will* like it here, huh Jim?"

"Yeah. Maybe . . . ."

The big house and the lawn looked good, and I was glad to see Jackie smiling. Nobody could take Mama's place, and I didn't understand what a foster mother was. But I'd give this place and the "nice Mrs. Ames" a chance.

"Please, could you tell me how a foster mother and a foster home work?" I looked up at the social worker. "We only had Mama, and she never expected to be dead in the hospital, so she never told us we'd live in a big house with other kids."

"Not now, James! We've already told you, so do try to at least appear glad to have the chance Mrs. Ames is giving you!"

Jackie grabbed hold of my hand as we started up the walk. A prim-looking woman in a starched dress and apron seemed to be the head of the house. A couple of other women stood nearby, also looking neat and stiff. We were led to the one who said, "My, you *are* big for your age, James! And you must be Jack. You boys were chosen from other applicants because I want to give my very *own* son, Patrick, some good companionship. Do you think you can be a good companion, James?

"And you, Jack, what about you? You and Patrick are the same age. Will you be a good companion to my *own* Patrick?"

Jackie didn't know how to answer and looked at me. I came to the rescue. "We've never been one of those what-you-said-before, but I am big for my age, and I can learn. I don't know if Jackie is old enough."

"Oh my goodness, James, you *are* droll! Did you hear that, ladies? Well, boys, come inside and let's see if we can find 'Patsy.'"

We were told where to put our small bundle of clothing, then led to a back door which looked out upon a huge yard. After the one-room apartment and the play area of Juvenile Hall, it looked good. I wanted to take off my shoes and run through the grass, but held back. *No way* was I going to act like a kid! I had to learn this new job—what was it called? Oh yes, a "companion"—so we could have a foster mother and home.

Maybe if I did it really good Jackie could stay with me. Maybe it wouldn't be so bad to work if we could have a chance to sometimes play together in the yard, just the two of us. Maybe even Patrick could play if he was going to have me as his companion. Maybe he needed someone special to take care of him because he was sick or crippled. I'd be good to him if he needed someone like that.

I wondered which of the six other boys in the pretty yard was the sick kid. I didn't see any crippled boy. What was a companion, anyhow? Things had a way of being told when the ones in charge were ready—and not before. This I'd learned very well at Juvenile Hall.

My thoughts were private as we walked into the yard. *Mama, I don't like this old lady Ames. I don't even know her! But I'll try to, Mama, and then I'll tell Jackie to try. You'd like the yard, Mama, and the grass! You said how it was back home where you lived when you were a little girl. You sang about a garden, and there is a flower garden here. But we don't have any man to be like a daddy to us, or even walk with us sometimes.*

"James and Jack, this is my very *own* Patrick! The other boys will just stay here, and you can get to know them later! Now, you three boys run along and get acquainted. And *don't* get dirty! We have rules here too, you know, and laundry takes a lot of work."

Patrick looked us over. "Hi! You only got to come here 'cause my mother wants me to have friends. She said you'll get to stay all the time, but the others go to school and then go home nights. How come your father and mother don't come and take you back home at night?"

"We came here to be what your mother said; we didn't come to talk. Jackie and me don't talk about our mother and father, so don't you, either. And don't *you* forget that, Jackie!"

"Okay, Jim!" Jackie's voice sounded relieved as he glanced first at me, then at Patsy, as we began to call him.

But Patsy wasn't satisfied with that. "*You* don't need to tell me, I'll ask my mother!"

That made me mad. I felt like hitting this boy who was so much smaller, but held it back. I called to Jackie, "Let's go! Last one to the tree is a sissy!"

I let him beat on purpose, then ran and ran until I almost dropped, hoping to get away from feelings that were driving me nuts.

Finally I dropped under the tree and stared up into the branches, speaking in a whisper to the bird nestled there. "You're a lucky bird, bird! You can go when you're ready, just fly away! And people don't tell you which tree to sit in, do they, bird?" I remembered a picture of a nest and a mama bird feeding her family. "I bet *you* don't have to be no companion to anyone to get a worm, do you, bird?"

Maybe Mrs. Ames didn't realize the needs of two small boys without a mother. I couldn't understand her. No matter how hard I tried to be good, I couldn't. It just wasn't in me to lie in bed at night and wish for Mama and a home of my own, then be good to a kid like Patrick. Especially since he had a beautiful home and a mother who saw to it that he had whatever he wanted.

Jackie soon joined me in some pretty rough games, then I'd

protect him and see to it that Patsy got beaten. I was big and didn't even try to be a good sport. Jackie and I would pick a fight with Patsy, then I'd beat up on him. Not really hurting him badly, just scaring him. Sometimes I'd tackle Patsy, then Jackie and I would both sit on him, threatening and holding him down until he would say, "I give up." We knew and were glad that Mrs. Ames would be upset when her *own* son was crying.

Many times she told us not to be so mean, but about the time Patsy thought sure his mother had shaped us up, we'd pounce on him again. I couldn't help my feelings of resentment—and at times real hatred—toward Patsy and Mrs. Ames. My strongest feelings weren't against Patrick, but I couldn't deal with the downright meanness of his mother. She was the enemy.

At no time did the woman offer us comfort or a chance to accept her as a replacement for our mother. Nor did any of the women who worked with her. We soon understood that if we didn't do as she, her staff *and* Patrick said, we'd be right back in Juvenile Hall.

To me Mrs. Ames was a phony, not only to the social worker, but to Patrick. She loved the money for keeping us more than she cared about her son's safety or happiness.

I've known many foster parents, and few make a profit if they do a good job. But we got as little to eat or wear as one could. We never felt the loving home atmosphere that the court intended for us. Yet, even with our needs barely met, we'd have learned to love that home if given a chance, for Jackie and I were not used to anything else. If only one person had spoken the words we so needed to hear—"You are loved."

Our only way to get to ol' lady Ames was through Patsy.

Ever since our mother had been attacked, Jackie and I weren't comfortable in the dark. At night I'd tough it out for Jackie, telling him not to be afraid. But he was not even near to overcoming this fear when Mrs. Ames learned of it. He was scared when alone in the dark; so she punished us by separation. For misbehaving (as I often would) I'd get whipped, and when Jackie was involved (which he usually was) he'd be locked in a closet somewhere in the house.

Jackie was scared and cried, but as I grew more calloused, I'd fight back.

"You won't make me cry, you ol' witch!" I'd brag. I could run faster than anyone and was growing taller and stronger every day. Mrs. Ames' meanness, Jackie's sadness, and my growing hatred met head-on on the Fourth of July.

What little boy never wanted a cap pistol—especially on the Fourth? Some friend of our foster home gave each of us a cheap little cap gun and a couple of boxes of caps. It was wonderful!

Soon we were all set to have a big celebration in the back yard. Jackie and I danced about playing cops and robbers. We let Patsy in on the fun, even forgot all about his mother! I twirled my little gun, showing off for the two smaller kids. That day I was—for a change—behaving.

Somehow Patsy dropped his pistol, and it broke. I tried to fix it. We needed his gun, too. The more noise, the better. But I couldn't repair it, so Jackie and I started playing again while Patsy went bawling to his mother. In no time, she marched outside to round us up and bring us indoors. This was just too much, even for a good kid like Jackie. "I'm *not* going in!" he sassed. "This is the Fourth of July, and I wanna shoot my gun!"

Mrs. Ames captured Jackie easily and hauled him into the house. I followed. "Turn him loose!" I demanded. Seizing the chance to get another cap gun, Patsy blamed Jackie for his misfortune.

"Liar, liar! Pants on fire! Lousy liar!" I yelled.

"There now, you boys don't deserve the guns anyhow.

Talking like that! You *both* need a lesson. Jack, give Patrick your gun this very minute!"

"I won't! I don't have to! . . . do I, Jim?"

"No! Here, give it to me! She can't catch me!"

In the scuffle, Mrs. Ames got Jackie's gun. "Now, Jack, into the closet where you can think over the trouble you get into by listening to James."

She whirled around and glared at me. "Go to your room. Stay there the rest of the day to think over your bad behavior!"

"I won't! And you let Jackie out of that closet right now or I'll . . . I'll kill you, you ol' witch! I hate you!"

Her face became red, she grabbed me and spun me around and put me into the closet with my brother, slamming the door. In hatred and fear we kicked, banged, shouted and screamed, begging in vain to be let out of the dark.

I knew it was wrong to say and do what we did, but I wasn't sorry.

"I'm so scared, Jimmy!" my brother whined.

"Nothing can hurt us, Jackie. Nothing is in the closet. We're safe. The ol ' lady'll have to let us out sometime." He clung to me, and I held him close while he cried himself to sleep. It was like the days when we were together with Mama. *Mama, what ever happened to you? Will we ever have a home again?*

I longed to hear her sing again about *The Man*, thinking that maybe He'd come and rescue us. But when I thought of Mrs. Ames, I began to hate again. Somehow I would get back at her. That ol' lady would be sorry the next time we tangled. I would win!

We were in the closet maybe four hours, long enough for Jackie to get sick, hot and sweaty. Alone in our room, he whined. "It just ain't fair, Jimmy! We didn't do anything this time. How I wish we had Mama again! Will we have to stay here forever? I wish we could run away."

Morning came, and we were fed. Trying to get on our good side, Patsy asked us if we wanted to play; he even offered to let us take turns using the two toy guns. I said, "Let's play cowboys and Indians."

My mind told me we shouldn't cause trouble, for I didn't want Jackie back in the closet. He didn't look so good to me, even yet. He was ready to play, though, and since we knew that cowboys had guns, I told Patsy to keep them. We'd be the Indians.

Indians dance—and we sure did! Feeling free, I glanced up to see Mrs. Ames at the clothesline. She smiled. I guess she thought our dancing and whooping was okay. When she returned to the house, I told Patsy to let me have his little pocketknife. Sooner or later either the cowboys or the Indians would have to win, and the prisoner would have to be captured and tied. He believed me. That surprised me. He handed over his knife right away.

Hollering and screaming like a savage, I approached the clothesline and cut off enough to tie Patsy to the "stake," a tree. But no stake was ever more real to any Indian as the game went on. I got Jackie to help hold Patsy and, as I whooped and danced round, the rope twirled around his body. Patsy, caught up in the game, looked excited and spellbound. We skipped and jumped toward the brush pile which the prim old ladies kept near the garden, and hauled some of the brush over to pile around the prisoner. I was a warrior, and Patsy was the enemy! He had to be burned so he wouldn't get free and tell other enemies where we were camped.

The make-believe kept getting more real. I sent Jackie to raid the kitchen, reminding him to be careful; there were enemies in there, too, who didn't like the red man. I told him to bring whatever he could for a night at the camp.

"And don't forget the matches!"

Before I knew it, a small box of matches was in my hand. A scheme to scare Mrs. Ames and Patsy quickly formed in my mind. I lit the brush, and a wisp of smoke began to rise. The early flickers of fire were far from the prisoner at first, but the rubbish rapidly caught. As the swelling flame swept closer, Patsy began to scream, "Mother! Help! Take me out . . . Mother!"

The terror in his voice brought me to my senses, and I looked at his face, so full of fear. I wanted to untie him but couldn't. The blaze around him was too hot. Afraid to go into the fire, and scared not to, I panicked and ran toward the street. Slowed somewhat by Jackie, I urged, "Faster, Jackie, we've got to get away!"

Suddenly one of the women who worked for Mrs. Ames grabbed us. We were slapped, jerked, and told over and over again how good we had had it. "And *this* is the thanks Mrs. Ames gets for taking you in!"

Somehow Patrick was rescued, but his legs were burned a little.

The juvenile authorities were immediately called, and we were back that very day in the place we had so longed to escape. This time I knew why, and decided maybe we weren't ever going to get along without trouble, especially me.

Chapter 4
THE "INCRIGIBLES"

"Terrific!" the investigator said, "Just what I need after the holiday. A couple of baby incorrigibles!" Jackie looked at me but neither of us spoke. We didn't know what that word meant, but we did understand her tone of voice.

"Well, say something! Whatever possessed you two, trying to kill a little boy by burning him alive?"

"We were only playing, then we couldn't stop the fire; we didn't mean to hurt him!" I protested. Jackie's eyes started to tear and I continued, "Honest, we didn't mean it!"

"Stop sniveling!" the investigator snapped. "If you're old enough to burn a kid alive, then grow up enough to talk about it, and in Heaven's name, tell the truth!"

I *had;* what more could be said? Jackie was still teary-eyed as the matron probed. "Mrs. Ames has already told us you've been jealous and *hated* her son since the day you arrived! That woman wanted to give you two a break!"

"She's a liar! She's mean! She locked us up in a closet and whipped us, and we didn't even do anything bad. And we didn't try to kill Patsy—we didn't!" I sassed angrily.

"All right, calm down. I've heard all about your temper fits, Jim, and this won't help. As for you, Jackie, I'm surprised at you! Mrs. Ames said you didn't seem like a kid who'd burn another one alive! Why did *you* get into this mess?"

Jackie stared coldly and said nothing.

"Well, I can see we won't get anywhere with you two today. I'll have to make my report to the Juvenile Court and see what we can arrange to straighten you out! Good Lord! Why do people have kids they don't teach anything to?"

This remark was made more to herself than to us, but I heard it and defended, "It ain't Mama's fault she's dead in the hospital!"

"A few more tricks like you just pulled and *you* may end up 'dead in the hospital'. Now, get out of here!"

We were taken to eat, but Jackie couldn't and I wouldn't. We didn't talk at the table and soon were sent to the playground, where we sulked by the fence.

"Maybe we are what that lady said, Jim—you know, 'incrigible'—we knew we shouldn't take matches. What is it going to do to us, Jim? Will we always be 'incrigible', now that we don't have no home no more?"

"Ah, forget it, Jackie! You know we didn't mean to hurt Patsy. We even kinda liked him. It was ol' lady Ames we hated. She's the one I'd like to burn!"

The thought gave me pleasure. I could see it all before my eyes, how she'd beg me to let *her* go. After awhile I thought of Patsy and said aloud, "We couldn't burn her up, Jackie. As big a sissy as Patsy is, he'd die without *his* mama!"

The authorities let us sleep in the same room this time, and that made us more comfortable. We followed the regular routine, being careful when any of the boys looked at us suspiciously. I hadn't forgotten that day in the shower room. Seldom was Jackie out of my sight.

We played some and I ate well, but Jackie looked tired and sick. One of the nurses told him to rest in the afternoons. As he'd lie in bed, I'd cheer him up with a book or game which was there for all to share. As the days passed, he grew more listless and feverish. One afternoon the nurse made me go out-of-doors while she took care of Jackie. When I was permitted to go back to our room, which we shared with other boys, Jackie was gone.

"He's been taken to the hospital," I was told.

The hospital! When Mama went to the hospital, it was the last time I'd seen or heard from her! "I wanna go, too, right now, *please*! I'm not supposed to ever leave him, and he needs me!"

I was told to calm down. But when I continued to beg, the lady in charge showed a spark of feeling. "Jackie had a high fever, Jim. He needed grown-ups—doctors and nurses. Don't worry; he'll get well," she smiled reassuringly.

But I didn't understand, or try to. "I want to be with Jackie! He's the only person I have left in the whole world. When will you bring him back?"

"We don't know. This is out of our hands, but he *will* get the best of care."

For the next few days I kept asking about my brother. He had a contagious disease, the authorities explained, and wasn't allowed to be with anyone except the people who were looking after him in the hospital. Still upset and angry over our separation, I became hard to handle. At night I'd tell myself that it wouldn't be like Mama, that we'd be together again. I'd make myself be good and not cause trouble; then in the daytime I'd grow more and more rebellious at not having him. He just couldn't be that sick!

Maybe the rebel in me would succeed where good boy Jimmy had failed. I gave them more and more problems. No one cared for me or my feelings; I would create all the trouble I could.

The administration authority sent for me one day after I had thrown food on the floor. "Well, Jim, since you're such a tough little customer, we've decided to send you to a place where all that energy can be put to good use," he spoke firmly. "You need to be tamed, and we've found just the place for it. Get ready to leave. And get set to work, young man! Where you're going, there are *men* to handle you! You may be big for your age, but they won't stand for the things you've put all of us through!"

"Good! Any place is better'n this dump!" I sneered. To myself I muttered, *Down with everybody! No one cares about me, so I won't care about them!*

I didn't ask about Jackie again while I was there. My pride wouldn't let me.

Chapter 5
"YOU'LL LEARN, KID"

It didn't take long to gather what few personal articles I had and be ready for my next juvenile camp. I still had no idea what a b— was; I was too proud to ask the kids who used that word; I only knew it would cause a fight, but it fit the man who had caused all the changes in my life. Had he been caught? Someday I'd find out . . . maybe.

I wished Officer James would answer some of my questions. Why hadn't I heard anything from Mama—or Jackie—since they'd gone to the hospital? I even thought a second about Dad . . . and *The Man* in the garden who had caused Mama to sing. Suddenly, I hated even Him! Where was He when I needed help? Someday I wouldn't need anyone—and, boy, I'd be glad!

Officer James came to see me off. He had kept his word and stayed in touch. He really did care, but had no authority to help me. How much I appreciated him, even then. Having no idea of behaving, I listened to him respectfully, as one would a friend.

"Jim, you're so young to be going to a boys' camp. Life hasn't been good to you so far—but listen, it *can* get better! Maybe I haven't shown it, but I do care what happens to you. I wish it wasn't like it is now, because I know how tough it can be on kids like you. Mixed in with others who are older and know every trick in the book. I've been told how you've acted, Jim, and it doesn't help, you know. But the ones you'll be with where you're goin'—how can I help you?"

The officer looked at me intently. "You don't even know what I'm talkin' about, do you?"

He was half right. I hadn't forgotten what had happened in the shower room, but there was still much I didn't understand.

One thing Officer James said stayed with me. "Well, can you believe me when I tell you that you can't win when you are outnumbered—and there will always be numbers, boy! There will always be fellas bigger 'n tougher, so don't go lookin' for a fight, do you hear me, Jim?"

"Yes, sir!" It was one of the few times I didn't resent the term. Mr. James shook my hand, then tousled my hair and grinned, "Good boy! If I ever get time off, I'll come and see you, okay?"

I nodded.

Riding in a station wagon to the camp, I thought about my talk with Mr. James. I'd first asked him about my mother. She was still in the hospital, was pretty sick but slowly improving. That explained why I hadn't seen or heard from her. Jackie, I learned, had polio. He, too, was getting better. Officer James told me there were "reasons" that I couldn't see either of them and, like it or not, I had to accept the facts. I would learn later the real reason we were kept apart. I was considered a bad influence on my brother, and the authorities believed it best that we stay apart.

Though younger than everyone else, I was bigger than many of the nine - through sixteen-year-olds at the camp. The setting was actually quite pretty, and I was glad for the change of scenery. It crossed my mind that maybe this wouldn't be such a bad place to wait for my family. Discipline, I soon would discover, was the uppermost thought in the minds of those in charge, and all the boys were there to be taught to obey.

Upon admittance, an officer showed me the grounds, pointing out where I'd be sleeping, eating and working. I'd attend school half a day and work the other half, he said. He explained my "program" in a tone which revealed he was just doing his duty. Fine with me. Who needed favors from a cop, anyway? I much preferred my own company, as one couldn't be sure who his friends were. My best choice was to stay out of trouble, stay alone, and just let the days go by till I could go home.

My first prison-type uniform was issued to me by another officer. We wore blue shirts and jeans during the week and a khaki shirt and pants for the weekend of special events. I never had anything "special" in all my time there, but some of the boys did. They had an honor and point system. You could earn the right to attend various activities.

Since the camp was still under construction, we had a lot of work detail. The machinery and tools looked interesting, but I didn't understand much about what was going on.

We were told to march everywhere we went unless it was a recreation period. The first time in line for the dining hall, I marched with the same attitude I'd had when playing soldier with Jackie. Tramp, tramp, tramp! I was enjoying it—and showed it because the boy in charge, who was much older than I, called out, "Tucker! Wipe off that smile. I don't stand for any kid-stuff in *my* line!" The make-believe sergeant was doing as he'd been told, but it was right then that I decided to buck this dumb system. Who cared about their silly points, anyway?

For the moment I obeyed orders and tried to appear grown-up, long remembering the embarrassment I suffered by the wisecracks of the others who whispered, "You'll learn, kid!"

After this incident, I became tense, always suspecting trouble just around the corner. As others would look at me, I would cringe. *What do they want of me? To do their work? To be "friendly," like in the Juvenile Hall shower room? These guys could even kill me!*

My mind flashed back to the attacker and to ol' lady Ames. I had to have a plan. The only thing I had going for me was my size. *That's it. I'll act tough and work hard. Maybe they'll let me alone.*

Although tough on the outside, I was unbelievably shy in speaking. One evening it showed. At dinner the boy in charge yelled, "Okay, Tucker, your turn to ask the blessing on the food!" I looked around at the others who appeared to enjoy my discomfort. Suddenly, the rebel in me took over.

"God bless this food; *now*, grab your forks and spoons and let's eat!" I shouted.

Because of this rudeness, I was ordered to leave the dining hall and stand at attention in a small punishment area of the compound. Just a small square, I could hear their smart remarks. *They will pay! I'll find a way to get even.*

The day finally came, but I hadn't planned it at all. It had been raining, and the march uphill to the dining hall in the muddy clay wasn't easy. Once at the top, I imagined how funny it would be if the whole string of clean, marching boys fell down! As the guy behind me heard my laugh, he swore, "What the h— you laughin' at, squirt?"

I whirled and kicked him in the shins hard enough to make him fall, tripping the boy behind him and so on down the line until most of them were in the mud! Looking down from the hilltop, I laughed long and loud. They were all my enemies!

"You shouldn' oughta done that, kid! Me 'n the gang are just gonna hafta teach you to grow up!" the first boy swore, wiping his hands on his pants legs.

The second voice was just as threatening. "Dummy up! Say

we slipped, see? We'll get to *him* later."

The gang chose a guy named Lloyd to get the job done on me. I'd been careful to avoid him since my first day at the camp. As the officer was showing me around, Lloyd had gotten close enough to wisecrack about how cute I looked.

During free time that evening, Lloyd walked up to me with some of his pals who had been downed in the mud. He put a strong arm around my shoulder, making it hard to draw away. I tried to wiggle free.

"Here's how to stand still, cutie!" Lloyd quickly pinned my arm behind my back. Then he patted me on my backside. "Oh, Jimmy, you and I are gonna be *real close* friends!"

His meaning was clear. The gang was laughing now, not me! I struggled, knowing that unless I downed this big guy, big trouble lay ahead.

"Relax, kid! Nice 'n easy now. I'm gonna let ya go—then you and me are gonna git acquainted." He looked at his pals, who enjoyed it all.

As soon as he let go, I swung and landed a fairly hard right to his shoulder. It hardly phased him.

"Go ahead, try to fight me, kid. Makes it interestin'—right, guys?" With that, he knocked me down with a hard punch on the chin and stood over me glaring.

"Now, you gonna be a good boy when Lloyd comes around?" I had no choice but to nod.

One of the guys in the crowd spoke up, "Stand clear! The little feller's in a hurry to go to the toilet. We wouldn't want him to mess himself, now, would we? Let's all make sure that don't happen."

I was taken by the hand, pulled to my feet and hurried into the restroom. The guys shoved, smacked, and undressed me until I was too afraid to break loose. Then it was the same as what happened at Juvenile Hall.

"If you stool on us," Lloyd growled after it was over, "you might be s'prised what *else* you'll git from us—only it'll hurt *more,* got me?" Left alone, I hurriedly dressed and returned to my barracks, determined to find some way to get even.

Hatred burned so deeply that I could easily have killed anyone who crossed me at that moment. Only the fear of never seeing Mama and Jackie again held me back. I laid awake all night scheming to get back at Lloyd. Finally, I thought of a plan. I'd be a winner or I'd die! What was the use anyhow? There was no fairy-tale Man in a garden to rescue me. I only had myself.

The next morning I marched to the mess hall as usual, but it was true when I told the guard that I felt sick and hadn't better eat. He excused me from chow, and I was either to turn out for work detail or go see the medic. On the way back to the barracks, I detoured a few feet into the tool shed, where I found a length of pipe and some electrician's tape. Going quickly to the barracks, I took off my long-sleeved shirt and taped the pipe to my right arm, then put my shirt back on. Later while everyone was involved in their work, I slipped away from my group and looked for Lloyd. Even at my husky size I was shorter than he; still, I had to fight and win. My heart was like cold steel. What I had planned he had coming!

Walking up to him, I acted real tough. "You still like an interestin' fight?"

"Well now, look who's showed up lookin' mad! You wouldn' hurt good ol' Lloyd, would ya, cutie?" He inched closer, as though to see just what a young kid like me had in mind. "Go ahead, start somethin' and you'll git what I told ya last night—only sooner!"

A group had gathered, and that suited me just fine. I stepped back a bit, then just as he stooped down to get his face closer to mine, I faked a left punch, then quickly followed with a hard right to the side of his head. The wallop of my right hand reinforced by the pipe flattened him. I whirled and ran at top speed as the others gasped in astonishment.

"Wow! Looka that!"

"Ol' Lloyd is really down!"

"Tucker really has a hard right hand! Gotta watch him!"

It felt good. I'd shown 'em! In a fair fight I never could have—but they didn't fight fair, so I had to go by their rules. No one ever found out how I'd downed Lloyd. From then on, it was going to be the other guy who got hurt, not me. I had learned how to survive.

For decking Lloyd I was dealt an unfair and undue punishment, probably even illegal for a child of eight: solitary confinement for fifteen days. Maybe it was just as well, from the standpoint of my safety. It took Lloyd a good while to recover from a bad headache and his grudge against me.

I was kept in a cell five by eight feet, furnished only by a cot and seatless toilet. Allowed outside under guard just one hour a day, I had lots of time to think. Because *I* got the isolation instead of the others, my hatred grew even faster. Still there was Mama and Jackie. She just couldn't stay in that hospital forever! Maybe if I really tried to do better, I could get out of this crummy dump, and we'd be together again.

But it was too late to cooperate. Once out of isolation, I was taken to the superintendent's office and told that the authorities had decided to send me back to Juvenile Hall. I kept disappointment to myself. *Who cares? They won't want me there either, so I'll be somewhere else in no time!*

Chapter 6
A GLIMMER OF HOPE

"Well, so *you* are James Tucker!" the matron said. "I hear you're quite a fighter. Your case has been assigned to me, and I think we ought to see what we can do to keep this file from growing. What do you think?"

I just shrugged and looked at her. She seemed to expect me to say something. "I found out I'm in Bakersfield," was all I could think of.

That was a good start, for then she explained that the Los Angeles and Bakersfield areas were cooperating in juvenile court systems and placements. I understood that well enough, but thought, *Bet they still don't want me in Los Angeles Hall.* In my mind that place had always been full of dirty guys, and I was glad not to be with them, too.

"From your file, I see that you have a mother, Molly Tucker, who has been in the hospital for a very long time. Almost two years! Also, you have a brother, Jack Tucker, who is presently at a boys' school for the handicapped. I suppose you knew he had polio, and his legs are crippled from that. But he *is* well now. Also, your father has not been in touch with you for many years—since long before you were first sent to Los Angeles Juvenile Hall. Is this all correct, James?"

"Yes, Ma'am, I guess so." I was glad Jackie was in school, but his being crippled made me sad.

"All right, *now* let's talk about your grandparents or any relatives from Oklahoma. Did you ever meet them? Did you ever visit them or did they ever visit you?"

"No, Ma'am, I only had my mother and Jackie."

"Well, do you have any friends, Jim? People who knew you from before?"

"Mr. James is my friend. He used to come and see me once in awhile."

"His name is in here, but he's left the department, so another officer is keeping in touch with you and your family. Did your mother ever have any friends or people who knew all of you before she was hurt? We don't know very much about you, so think about it a while."

"Some ladies cared for me and Jackie while Mama worked."

"Well, since you have been so cooperative, I've decided to give you some good news! After such a long time in the hospital, your mother is recovering! That means she will get well in time. You've hardly smiled since we've been talking. How do you feel?"

"Could I go there? Can I see her? Can I see Jackie, too, in that school?" The news *was* exciting. I felt happy. Eager.

"Slow down, Jim, I only know what's on this paper! It does say, however, that children may not visit the hospital. That's a rule in most hospitals, so don't let it upset you."

"But I want to see them! Please?"

"I said you weren't to get excited! So you may return to your room, and we'll talk later." As she spoke, the little con in me took over. I took a slow, deep breath and changed my expression.

"Okay, I'm not excited now. Will you please tell me more about Jackie, Ma'am? You said he's crippled. How did he get crippled? Will he come to this Hall and be with me when he finishes that school?"

"Now, Jim, you are going too fast for both of us!" the matron smiled. "Let me try to explain. The disease called polio has affected his legs; he can't walk as he used to. But he can use crutches. He *is* well except for that, and he's doing fine at the school. He'll have to stay there for quite a while yet, I'm afraid. Along with the education and training, Jackie gets good medical checkups."

She sighed and sobered. "I think I'll tell you now. The judge has ordered that, until you both are older, you will *not* see each other. You know why, Jim. You were never a good influence on your brother. This separation may keep him out of more trouble."

"But he's my brother! I'd never do anything to hurt Jackie. What did I do? We only have each other and now he needs me more than ever. Who said he was bad around me? If it was ol' lady Ames, she's a liar! Mama said I'm to look after him!"

"Now, that's *enough*! It's decided. And you *are* too emotional, so no more talk today! I wanted to give you good news, not upset you. Go back to your dorm, now." Her firm voice was clear. No use arguing with her further. . . .

My parents' story is not long. Mother and Dad were very young and wild in their own ways when they met in Oklahoma. The depression was over, and they were teenagers who wanted to see more of life and the world away from home.

My father was a handsome, showoff kid. Mother was beautiful and thought he was a real man! They made an attractive couple: Dad had dark hair and eyes, and Mama was fair with bright red hair and green eyes. Both loved good times and excitement. Since they had so much fun together, they decided that they were in love. And maybe they were.

Because of an old feud between their families, Dad and Mother were forbidden to marry. They ignored this and eloped, becoming outcasts. Never again were they welcome among their own people. This could be the reason none of them came to get Jackie and me.

My father was a chef and did quite well at it. He was not afraid of hard work, but began to drink and gamble heavily. At first, Mama didn't mind; she even joined him.

My dad became *the man* in cards. He was quick and could clean up a bundle fast. He convinced Mama that they could be rich in a hurry, so in the first few months of their marriage she'd help him raise a stake by singing in a cocktail lounge or by selling something they owned. For a while they had what they wanted—excitement, night life and each other.

The more Dad mixed gambling with booze, the more he lost. Either they had plenty or almost nothing. At the time Mother was pregnant with me and was often ill. She asked Dad to stop the gambling and drinking, to settle down and work for a living. But gambling had too great a grip on his life.

They were headed to "somewhere," with nothing of their own but an old car and a few dollars, when I was born. She gave birth to me in that old car, and probably had poor care, if any. They registered my birth before I was named, so my birth certificate says only, "Baby Boy Tucker."

Dad took Mother to an apartment and somehow paid the rent, but they fought all the time and, in time, separated. She took care of me and worked. Dad returned some time later, staying long enough for her to become pregnant with Jackie. He couldn't keep away from gambling and drinking and was restless to be on the move. He left the three of us right after Jackie's birth, and we never saw him again. Dad eventually died of alcoholism.

Mother worked as a cocktail or dinner waitress and was popular as a singer in the Los Angeles restaurants where she served. With her lovely voice and beauty, she managed to support her habit of pills and liquor and still take care of two sons.

If Dad ever got word of what happened to the beautiful girl he married and his two sons, I never heard about it. But I'd like to think that it would be something he'd regret.

My life in Bakersfield held just one glimmer of hope. I was still a kid with a dream. I *still* wanted Mama, Jackie and me together again, somehow . . . somewhere!

Chapter 7
OL' EBO AND THE WITCH

Sitting in my dorm, I was mad and confused. I was getting the dirty end of the stick and helpless to do anything about it. I still didn't know what hospital my mother was in or which school my brother attended.

Most of the other kids had visitors, but I hadn't had anyone come to see me since Mr. James. Now he was no longer showing up. Who was the other cop that was supposed to take his place? Would he come by and become my friend?

Time passed slowly while my feelings of jealousy, rejection and bitterness grew, and turned more inward every day. The Christmas holidays were the loneliest, especially when the decorations went up and the packages began to arrive. It was unbearable to watch the happiness of others.

While I was in this frame of mind, my first visitor arrived. *Maybe it's the new cop,* I thought, walking excitedly to the visiting area. *Maybe it's Mama or . . . Jackie.*

Just as I was about to step through the now open security door, the duty officer smiled, "Your mother is here, Jim."

When I entered the room, a lady was seated with her head turned slightly away from me. She was wearing a coat and a hat, the brim hiding part of her face.

"Mama?"

"Yes, Jim, it's me." She turned, stood up, and held out her arms to me. Because of my height, I saw it full on. Her face! A mass of scars and scar tissue, and on one side was a huge, sunken hole. It made me sick.

"You're not my mama! You're *not* my mama! I hate you! Go away!" I ran to the locked door, crying and yelling, "Let me in! I want back in!"

The strong hands of the new cop who'd stood off to the side all the while took hold of my shoulders and turned me around. "Stop it, Jim. Right now! Your mother's had a lot of surgery on her face. She's been through a living hell. Now, you go over there and talk to her!"

"I can't! I can't! Don't make me!" I sobbed.

Mama had turned her face away, and she also was weeping. "Take me out now, *please*." Officer Conway let go of me and returned to her. His arms wrapped comfortingly around her, she buried her face against his chest. "It's okay, Molly, I'm with you."

To me he spoke softly and understandingly. "Go on back in, kid, and don't worry about your mother. I will be looking after her."

Somehow that heavy door opened and closed behind me. My dreams were smashed.

The time at Juvenile Hall dragged now. In the most unexpected times, especially at night, I'd see the face of the scarred lady, but would never accept her as my mother. Mama was beautiful. . . .

It was several years before I saw her again. By then the scar tissue had faded, the swelling and redness was cleared, but she still was pathetically disfigured.

Because of her marked face and my rejection, Mother had

every reason in the world to wonder what would become of her. During one of those times, between plastic surgeries, she called upon a fortuneteller named Fay Kane. To her, Mama poured out her bewilderment, sadness and loneliness. She told all, but to a woman whose very soul was scarred deeper and far worse than Mama's face.

Exactly how or why it happened I never learned, but Molly Tucker signed Consent to Adopt forms, and I was released from Bakersfield Juvenile Hall to Fay Kane, a con artist by reputation.

Appearing in the visitor's room, this strange woman was leaning on her walking stick. Her first words were right to the point. "Hi! I'm your new Aunt Fay!"

"No, I don't have no aunts."

"Well, you have now! I was watching you on the playground. You look big and healthy, and you need a home—so I'm taking you to live with me." Her green eyes squinted as she hobbled up to me and peered into my face.

Fay Kane was crippled and slightly hunchbacked. To me she looked old, probably around sixty-five. Her dress was clean but not fancy, and her stringy hair was pulled back into a knot; some of the side ends were loosened as though by wind, making her appear more unattractive.

I felt self-conscious as she walked around me—like I'd seen people in the movies do when they were dickering over a horse. She looked like the witch that she was—even before I knew about her black "arts."

I'd been in custody of one type or another for so long, I'd learned not to react to strange people and situations. *Who said I'm gonna live with you,* I thought.

"You *are* the Tucker boy, aren't you?"

"Yes, Ma'am."

"Well, whadaya say? You ready to leave here?"

"Maybe. Who says I can?"

"Look, boy! I've talked to the right people. It's legal if I want you. I need a big, strong boy around my place. I run a tourist camp. You come and help me, and I'll help you. 'T won't be fancy, but you're just the one I want. I've asked all about you, and I like a kid with spunk. You've got it, and you'll need it to work with me in my business. . . . Well?"

"You mean I'll work for you, and you'll give me a home?" It sounded too simple, even for a child who'd gotten an early knowledge of life.

"Beats juvenile detention, don't it?"

I didn't answer.

"Anyway, I'm a lonely ol' gal, I really am! I need someone around to keep me company, too. I will be an aunt to you, Jimmy."

I hated being called "Jimmy" by her. Only Jackie and Mama could call me that. She went on talking, and I kept quiet. Her hand reached out and she forced me to look into her squinty eyes. "I need someone to love and you *will* grow to love me, too!" She walked toward the door, then turned to give me one last chance to speak.

"Workin' part sounds okay. When you comin' after me?"

"Now. I'm here *now*, and I mean to take you with me."

She really meant it. It was just that simple. We were ushered before an authority, a paper was signed, and I was told to go with Mrs. Kane, that she now had charge of me. If I stayed out of trouble, she could be my adopted mother! Aunt Fay and some man who may have been a judge shook hands. Again I felt like a horse. Part of a deal!

Our first stop was a classy restaurant. The menu was hard for me to read, but she helped me order a huge meal for us. It was the first time I ever ate in a restaurant, and I was impressed. Especially about leaving a tip. Imagine being able to give a gift to someone just for handing us our food!

"Slow down, Jimmy. You're not on a schedule," she laughed. I listened and ate as she explained *her* program for my life. It involved school, which didn't thrill me. But the idea of riding a school bus sounded like fun, and there were other kids around to get acquainted with, boys and girls I'd have for friends. I wondered what it would be like to have a friend.

"Now, Jimmy, you'll need some school clothes and an outfit for when you need to dress up," she chattered, ignoring my obvious amazement.

I was allowed to choose what I wanted, and price seemed to be of no concern! My wonder grew every time she took out that roll of bills from her old-fashioned handbag. By her gifts she won my confidence.

"How did you really come to get me, Aunt Fay?" This time, it was her turn to be surprised that I knew she hadn't told the whole truth.

She would only answer, pleasantly enough then, "I saw you, found out all about you, and I chose you over the others."

I liked that lie. It was what I needed to hear, anyway. "Thanks for all the things, Aunt Fay."

"You're welcome, Jimmy dear—and remember, you do right by me, and there's more where these came from."

Being a normal kid, I dreamed of what to ask for next. Having seen her money, I decided to make sure she lived up to her promise.

The bus ride home was relaxing, and I thought of the trolley rides with Mama. For the first time, I could accept the scarred lady as Mama—and wondered why she couldn't have had Aunt Fay's money. It seemed unfair: She wasn't pretty any more and didn't come to take me home. In spite of my vow to get rid of the dream of *The Man*, I couldn't help talking to Him in my thoughts. *Since You didn't come and get me, I'll just go live with this ugly old Aunt Fay. At least she wants me.*

When the bus let us out, we started walking. "Are you married, Aunt Fay?" I asked hopefully. "Will I have any uncles? One of the kids at the Hall has six, and they used to take him fishin' and to the circus . . ."

"No, Jimmy, no uncles. And we don't need any. Just you 'n me. An' a cat an' a dog. Wait'll you meet them." She laughed strangely.

I'd thought it would be nice to live in a house again and not have to feel afraid. *Sure Aunt Fay is old and kinda ugly, but at least she wants me. And she did buy me a lot of things.* My thoughts continued until she told me we were home.

Home was a small cabin, not what I'd expected from a woman with all that money. Still, it was neat enough: a nice kitchen with all appliances, a bathroom and a larger area which was a combination sitting room and bedroom. Aunt Fay leaned her cane against a large, comfortable chair and walked over to a small table on wheels. The table held her crystal ball and underneath was a coal black cat.

She talked to the cat as she would a person. "Ebony, this is Jimmy—you know, the boy I told you was coming to live with us." The cat strutted to me and circled around my feet, reminding me how Aunt Fay had looked me over earlier that day. Suddenly, Ebony arched his back and hissed. His green eyes glared into mine, and I noted that they were the same color as Aunt Fay's. Furthermore, there was strength in both, as though either Ebony or Aunt Fay could pin me to the wall with a stare. I made up my mind not to get into a staring match with ol' Ebo, as I soon called him.

Aunt Fay seemed to enjoy the action between us, as she briefly sat and Ebony jumped into her lap. "Open the door and call the dog, Jimmy."

His name was Waif. We became friends, but he was loyal to Aunt Fay and always stayed close to the cabin. Ebo seemed indifferent and completely unthreatened by Waif, and the dog never crossed that cat. Neither did I. There was something evil about him.

It was late by the time all of us had a glass of milk, so Aunt Fay told me to get into my new pajamas—or just sleep in the raw, as I wished. With that said, off came her dress, slip, corset, shoes and stockings. Soon all she wore was her old-fashioned, rayon underpants, all of her fat sagging, all of her wrinkles showing. She had let her gray, straggly hair down and was gazing at me with piercing green eyes. I didn't want to stare at her, but I hadn't been around a woman without all her clothes on except Mama. Looking down at the packages on the floor, I wondered which one had the new pajamas in it.

"Well, c'mon, what're you waitin' for?"

"Where are my new pajamas, Aunt Fay?"

"Tomorrow. Do without them tonight."

"But, where do I sleep, Aunt Fay?"

"Right here in this bed with me." The sound of her laugh reminded me of ol' Lloyd. "And my other little sweetheart, Ebony, will watch over us from the foot of the bed." She put the cat in his new place and motioned for me to get into bed. I obeyed. Snapping off the light, she crawled in beside me, close. "Now, just relax, little fella. Told you I was just a lonely, old lady and needed someone to love." She began to rub my back, and feel all over my body.

As long as I lived with Fay Kane, I had everything I asked for except a room or a bed of my own.

Chapter 8
SPIDERS, LIZARDS AND TOADS

The sleeping arrangement wasn't the only thing strange at Aunt Fay's. There was a weird attachment between her and ol' Ebo. Also, the way Waif played second fiddle to a cat was unusual. Aunt Fay talked to Ebo about everything, and to Waif about his "place," mostly. They seemed to respond as humans, especially the cat. Although she was good to me in every way, I felt she was training me like one of her animals for my "place."

Aunt Fay's answer to everything was money. Often I'd notice other kids with their parents, and see how they sent them off to school with a hug, or walked hand in hand. The other mothers attended school meetings or sent cookies for special treats. Several times I tried to talk Aunt Fay into this sort of relationship. Her answer was always the same: "Here's a dollar; go get us some ice cream." I knew that was that.

My ninth birthday was celebrated with a party in Aunt Fay's yard. It was the first one I'd ever had, and it made me feel important, even special. I enjoyed having the finest clothes and the most spending money of any of the kids in my grade. Unhappy memories of Juvenile Hall and of the attack on Mama were fading.

Life with Aunt Fay seemed good—and interesting, in odd ways. I enjoyed more freedom than ever, gladly raked the leaves, got the mail from the box by the road, took out the trash, and fed good, faithful Waif. One day Aunt Fay explained that it was time to learn her "ancient arts," as she called them. Some day I could have it all, she said, but I had to want it.

I was too young to think seriously of learning witchcraft and spiritualism. Or reading the cards, making charms, and magic dolls. Yet all these were strangely fascinating to me, especially her crystal ball and what she told clients that she saw. I was allowed to sit in the kitchen with the door closed while she gave her customers their readings, provided I kept very quiet. Naturally, I eavesdropped and peeked through the old-fashioned keyhole. Aunt Fay warned that if I dared to reveal anything that went on in her house, she'd kick me out. I knew she meant it and made a game out of keeping her secret.

The things I saw and heard were astonishing. When a knock on the door sounded, she would take on a dignified manner as she went to answer it. Then she would speak very quietly as she invited the caller or callers to come in. The visitors had her complete and undivided attention. She never failed to have a ready answer, no matter what the problem or situation.

The sounds I'd hear coming from her weren't like the sharp, often vulgar words and tones she used most of the time. When her voice changed, I peeked to make sure it was Aunt Fay talking.

She'd say something like this: "Oh, my dear, I *know* the answer for you is in the cards. Let me draw the drapes so I can concentrate. I'm *sure* I'll get something to help you. Now, keep faith in me, never doubt my powers."

The table with the ball, where the cat lay underneath on the rug, would be rolled over to her comfortable chair, and Ebony would again settle himself at her feet under it.

Then she'd say something like, "I don't charge. I can only

accept gifts, otherwise I will lose my powers to help others like yourself." With that, a bill would be placed on the table. Then a ready word would seem to be just what the customer needed or wanted to hear. Encouraged by the client's approval of her powers, she'd suggest, "Shall we look into the crystal ball to see if there's more?" A reply and more money on the table prompted more words. Often people would be sold a charm or doll to further help with their problems.

Aunt Fay held a seance regularly for willing clients. She arranged folding chairs in a small circle, placing herself, the crystal ball, and Ebony in the middle. I was allowed to be present when these occurred, and was again warned never to interrupt.

I never did know how or from where the voices we heard were brought to our ears. I do know that the people asked questions or for messages from the dead before the lights were put out—and they received answers and messages. Sometimes more than they asked. The strange voices represented male and female and included those of children.

After the seance, when the lights were back on, large numbers of bills were again placed on the table. She'd allow the group time to settle down after marveling over what they had received and thanking her for helping. Then she'd say something like, "My dears, I *am* drained. I apologize, but I must rest now. Do return again, and I shall gladly intercede on your behalf." As she'd appear to be in need of sleep, everyone would leave.

Aunt Fay always introduced me as her adopted son, who would some day carry on when she was "on the other side." I knew better than to correct this idea.

Waif would walk them to their cars and often receive a friendly word. "My, even her dog is wonderful." When the customers were gone, her voice and manner were as coarse as before they had arrived. She was again Aunt Fay.

Many of the cars which came and went were big and fancy. I was impressed, yet puzzled, at the types of persons who called. Among her followers were such prominent people as judges, lawyers and police officers. I heard her counsel on such matters as money investments, buying cars or property, job affairs, health and happiness problems, and how to find a lover or get someone to leave his husband or wife.

Aunt Fay also asked and received information from influential people about many things. I never understood it all, but there was somehow an exchange of favors. Politics were discussed and charms and dolls exchanged. It was clear to me that Fay Kane was influential in many things in Bakersfield.

I enjoyed the times Aunt Fay took me "collecting." She pointed out certain wildflowers and weeds, as well as leaves, bark, spiders, lizards, frogs, toads, bugs, sea shells and soft stones. She kept many colors of cloth on hand and sterilized the items we collected by steaming or putting them in boiling water. All were used for making charms.

As she chanted some strange sounds and words, using certain body and hand movements, she would use an instrument to crush certain items. They were combined in exact proportions and poured upon the small squares of colored cloth. Each was tied with string or narrow ribbon to resemble a sachet and placed in a drawer. Her eerie laugh caused chills to go down my spine as she sometimes cackled, "Whoever gets the result of this one will wish he hadn't!" She made other charms to bring good. "Now, with this one my friend can have money. All he wants! And we'll get *our* share when he does," she'd chuckle. Some were about love, a lover, or a home for a love nest. "I got somethin' for everybody, Jimmy."

One evening she suggested, "Let's use your Ouija board, Jimmy dear, and give you a spelling lesson. Then before bed, we'll have tea and I'll read the leaves for you. If you don't have questions, I do. Let's see what life is going to bring us."

I went for the board, and she rolled out the table. "That's right, Ebony, you can help us play, too." As we sat with our knees touching, she put ol' Ebo in my lap.

"It's long past time you two became friends. Now, you stay there, Ebony. I've told you, you'll need Jimmy to carry on our work."

He stayed, but he stopped purring and sank his claws into my legs just enough to spoil my concentration. The board didn't work, and she gave up in disgust.

"It's your fault!" she spat. "If you would only get in tune with Ebony, I could teach you some things."

I'll be in tune with no cat, I muttered inwardly. *Least of all try to love him.*

"He's okay, but we just ain't friends like you are," I said aloud.

She sighed and looked upset, tired and very old. "Stay there, Ebony!" She got up and switched out the light, leaving just a small beam showing from the kitchen through the slightly open door. Barely able to see her outline, I wondered what was coming next. She assumed the soft, sweet tone reserved for her clients and said, "Now, dear, forget Ebony is on your lap. Just relax and he will, too."

Sure enough, he did. "Now, Jimmy, say what I tell you to say."

"Okay."

"Oh, thou Black Prince of Darkness, made manifest in the beautiful Ebony, make me to be in tune with you through him and Aunt Fay. Then give me your miracle-working power, and I will give you my soul."

"No!" I shouted fearfully. "I won't be in tune with no cat. He hates me! I won't sing or anything with him."

I didn't dare remain in the room. As I ran out the door and down the road, she sat in the dark soothing the cat.

Under the shelter of a tree, I wondered if Aunt Fay would keep me. When the cabin was in total darkness, Waif loped over and put his head into my lap, whining softly as I put my arms around his neck. Somehow he was on my side and had to show it at least this once.

"Jim-my! Come in now, Jim-my!" It was getting chilly, so I responded to her still pleasant voice. "You're cold and I've made tea for us. Sit on the floor by me, and I'll hand you a cup." Cup in hand, I watched Aunt Fay settle slowly into the big chair, which was hers alone.

"It's hard in life, Jimmy." She was continuing with her pleasant voice. "You're going to have to make some choices soon. Someone will show up one of these days to check up on you—from the court, you know."

"No, I didn't know. Are you planning to keep me?"

"Well, that depends on what *you* tell them. I can see in the leaves here in your cup, dear, that you only need a little more time to grow up. I'm only your Aunt Fay now, but as the years go by, I'll become your sweet mama—and honey, you'll always be my little sweet-pea!" She sounded possessive, and her tone now made me feel frustrated, even angry.

"No! I have a mama! It ain't her fault what happened! And I won't be no kind of flower sissy; you can't make me!"

Feeling tears in my eyes, I darted again into the chilly night to hide them, running down the road for the canal bank where the kids often played and toward my favorite cave.

Suddenly, I bumped into someone. "Wait a minute; you're too young to be out tonight without a coat. Let me talk to you." The voice spoke with gentle authority. I stopped and turned to look back. It was an older black lady. She pulled a sweater out of her shopping bag. "Both of us'll feel better if you borrow it, chile. You can bring it to me later." I grabbed the sweater without a word.

"You're all upset now, ain'tcha? It's all right, no need to talk. Tell you what, when you git ready jes bring it to the little house at the end of Reedy Lane, off of Cottonwood Road. My name's Katie, and I lives there all alone."

Thankful for the sweater, I went to the cave and crawled in for a good cry. Thoughts of Mama, Jackie, even *The Man* who was only make-believe, crept into my mind. In time I ambled back to the cabin. The door was unlocked and Waif didn't bark. If Aunt Fay heard me, she never let on when I crept into bed. Katie's sweater was safe back in the cave.

In a few days the investigator from the court came, and we talked. "Are you happy with your new home?"

"Yes," I lied, fearing Aunt Fay would send me back for saying otherwise. Besides, I'd never had so much money. That part of my life was okay. Then, too, I had just found a new interest that made everything look better—drinking wine and beer down on the canal bank with some other kids.

Aunt Fay kept me busy with odd jobs, all the while reminding me how she had taken me in and that I had more money than any other kid my age. I could repay her by carrying on the work and providing for her when she got too old, she said. The money part made sense even to my young mind, but the rest seemed complicated. She had a ready reply to my objections.

"Jimmy, grow up! You can do anything you want to if you'll

try. You're smart and you're big, so you appear older. Anyhow, if I say you're ready, you're ready—and I say you are ready to learn my powers, the sooner the better."

"Well, do I hafta do all that stuff—like look into the ball, and read cards, and talk to the dead people?"

"Not yet, but you should begin to learn. There's a power of light and a power of dark. You decide if you want power. Remember I said I'd give you anything. Well, I get it all with my powers!" Bothered by my silence, she frowned. "Well, don't I?"

"I like power all right, Aunt Fay. I just don't know if I could remember all the charm recipes, and see things in the ball or tell it all like you do." I thought of those strange voices which seemed to come from her mouth during the seances. "Besides, I'm too young. No one would believe in me."

"You leave that to me! When Fay Kane says you have power, you'll have it! Just like I got it. The Dark Prince is ready and waiting for you."

"You said there are two powers. Will I have both?"

"Of course not, stupid. Do you see the moon and the sun at the same time? You have to choose. I can only give you what I got."

"You keep talkin' about that Dark Prince, Aunt Fay. Where does he live? I never see him. When does he come around here?"

"That's not for you to understand. I can sure see you understand about the money, though, so you'd better choose the best way to get it. Ask the Dark Prince to open your mind so I can teach you quickly. Ask him to let me give you the same powers I have. You don't have to see him. He's here."

"Okay, guess I better. But can I do it later? I promised to meet some kids down by the canal," I lied.

The annoyance showed in her voice. "Then go! I'll need your complete attention when you're really ready. And he'll insist on it." As I went for my jacket, she swore, ". . . and get back early!"

None of it made sense. Why did I have to run out? I'd found one of her love charms in my underwear drawer, and it had made me feel weird, too.

I headed for the cave to get Katie's sweater and return it to her. Hurrying toward Reedy Lane, my thoughts turned toward the Dark Prince and those piles of bills laid on that little table for me. Maybe I *could* learn the powers after all; at least the money would make it worth the effort.

I didn't think Katie would know me, but when I held out her sweater, she really seemed pleased to see me.

"Come in, chile! You didn't need to hurry to bring it, but you been on my mind. No, honey, more den that! Katie knew you was one troubled chile."

I stepped in.

"What's your name? Here, sit a spell. I don' git much company, but I got a big homemade apple pie. I'll git it. You sit."

In no time she was back across the room, and I was eating the best pie I'd ever tasted.

"Well, I been agoin' on, and I still don' know my new friend's name."

"Jim Tucker."

"Don' know no Tuckah's. Your folks jus' move here?"

"No, Ma'am. Fay Kane adopted me from the Juvenile Hall."

"Ohmigawd! So you are the boy Miz Kane took in. She the one upset you the other night, I 'spect."

I nodded.

"Don' mean to talk so much, chile, but I knowed before you need a friend, now I know it more. My Jesus tol' me."

She watched me take another bite, then went on. "Miz Kane,

she's old, and so am I. But she got a troubled mind, young Jim Tuckah. I know her from way back. Don' you say nuthin' for it wouldn' be right. But I want to say somethin' to you. Sometime, maybe lots of times, you gonna need someone to come to so you can jus' rest—I wants to help you. Good Book says we s'posed to tend the garden—but you don' know 'bout that."

I just shook my head and accepted another piece of pie. "I rake leaves and help with Waif. He's her dog, and the cat is mean. But I think about a garden and a Man sometimes. I never talk about it though."

It sounded childish to speak of that, so I got busy with the pie again.

When the piece was gone and I sat back, Katie smiled, "You best run on back to the cabins now. Younguns like you need to git in early, and don' make yourself no more trouble if you can help it."

When I put on my jacket and went to the door, she reached for my hand, smiled, and said something no one else had ever said to me. "You need to know I been a-prayin' for you, Jim Tuckah. I'm not gonna s'plain 'cause you won't understand, but you need to know it. And you need to know now for sure I mean to keep on a-prayin' for you. But it's our secret, Jim, right?"

I shook her hand and grinned. "Right."

How did Katie know I liked to make a game of secrets? I knew nothing of prayer or of her Jesus, as she'd called Him. Yet I liked this lady. As I stepped out into the early evening darkness, she called, "And Jim Tuckah, my door is nevah locked. You evah need help, jus' you remembah, I don' lock my door."

Aunt Fay had customers when I got home, and she never

seemed to have time for the instructions we'd discussed after that. Her business picked up, and I was glad she was too busy.

I appeared agreeable enough to make Aunt Fay believe I'd be learning her arts and looking out for her in older years so that she would let me be with my friends more. At least I called them that.

The canal bank wasn't far from our cabin, and the other kids and I often met there to play among our caves. We'd built them by digging holes, then covering the tops with boards. Inside, they were cozy and quiet.

A wino usually lounged in the area, and I'd get him to buy some beer or wine and cigarettes for us. After getting what we wanted, I'd give him the price of a cheap bottle, then head for the caves.

We boys would go into our dens, mostly in pairs, especially if we had a girl with us. There we smoked, drank, and felt each other's bodies—boys or girls. Looking, touching and giggling quietly so no one would hear us was typical of most youth where I lived. It was a free feeling to be just a little drunk and naked, especially with a girl.

The kids enjoyed my company and all that my spending money could buy, but I felt unpopular at school. Always the smart aleck, I did anything to disrupt my class, mostly to get attention. I teased the little girls by pullling their hair, or putting their braids in the old-fashioned ink wells we didn't often use. I made fun of their paper dolls and destroyed a few. I laughed when they cried, and made fun of everything they enjoyed. I cheated at marbles and was a bully when none of the boys wanted to fight. I could get any one of them down, sit on him and make him say, "I give up." Yet I wanted to be liked for myself, not for what I could give along the canal.

One day I turned my white mice loose in the classroom, and

it was great fun to watch the girls and Miss Halsey scream for the boys and me to catch them and put them back in the box. Other times I put a garter snake and a lizard in Miss Halsey's desk. Sometimes I'd bring a frog or toad, and I always had a good supply of spiders or bugs after "collecting" for Aunt Fay.

I called my teacher "Miss Jelly Belly" to everyone, except her, of course. Short and fat, she would wheeze and sputter when she laughed or became excited. The rolls of fat around her middle shook like jelly.

Not feeling well, I was quiet in school one day, so another boy decided to cause a disturbance. He made a small paper wad, stuck some pins through it, then fashioned a slingshot out of a rubber band. While Miss Halsey had her back to the class putting her problems on the board, he pulled back and the pins went right to her rump.

The eraser went one way and the chalk another, while Miss Jelly Belly looked like she was trying to climb the blackboard. All of us howled, but our teacher was mad. I'd never seen her so upset. "Stop laughing this instant!" she screeched.

Miss Halsey grabbed the thick ruler and headed toward me. The others stopped laughing, and I wanted to, but just couldn't.

"Hold out your hand, Jim Tucker."

"No, I didn't do anything this time."

Without hesitating, she grabbed me firmly by the hair of my head and yanked me from the seat. "Liars don't belong in my class. I've taken enough from you; now you can sit in the principal's office."

Led by my hair to the main office, I was angry that she didn't believe me. As we left the room all of the kids were whooping and hollering. I thought they were making fun of me, and my pride was hurt.

In the principal's office, I visualized each kid I'd teased or cheated. I had been embarrassed. *Well, I'll just have to get even,* I muttered, spending the rest of the school hours figuring how to do it.

For the first time in my life I was with kids who hadn't ganged up to whip me. In time I fully expected to be popular and run the gang at school—at least those my age—and no school teacher was going to make a patsy out of *me* and get away with it.

The solution came. I'd just have to shoot her.

Chapter 9
ON THE RUN

Toward the end of the day Miss Halsey came to ask me to apologize.

"No. I didn't do it. I told you and you wouldn't believe me, so I'm going to kill you."

Angry, she called the principal out to talk to me. I warned him to let me alone or I'd kill him, too. The physical ed teacher was a strong man who could handle me, so he was called to give me a hard spanking. "Now you get on the bus, go home, and don't return until you intend to behave in school!" he ordered.

At home, I stayed indoors with Aunt Fay and was quiet. She didn't question me, and we spent the evening as usual. I was making a plan. I'd seen Aunt Fay's pistol, a very pretty chrome .38 automatic with a pearl handle. I knew where the shells were, but where was the gun?

The next morning I asked for something special for breakfast that I knew wasn't in the house. Aunt Fay often went early to the store near her tourist cabins so, as she was preparing to leave, I set my trap.

"Aunt Fay, I had a dream last night. You know that pretty pistol you have with the pearl handle? Well, I dreamed you lost it or something. Did you?"

"Not that I know of." I said no more.

As she continued getting ready, I watched her every move. When she went into the other room to get her purse, I peeked through the keyhole, as I often did. Bending over to pick up her purse, she quickly lifted the mattress to check on the gun. My plan had worked on a real pro!

After she had gone, I got the gun and took all three boxes of shells, storing them in a shoe box which I hid in the bushes. When Aunt Fay returned, I told her I was feeling better, ate breakfast, then left for school as usual, picking up the box as I ran toward the school bus stop.

All the kids wanted to know what was in it. I made a game out of it, saying it was a secret. The game continued on the school yard where I was able to outrun those who persisted in looking into the box. In a hiding place, I put a few shells in my pocket, hid the rest, and tucked the loaded gun into my belt under my jacket. Aunt Fay always kept the weapon cocked and loaded.

Running back to the others, I passed the empty shoe box to another boy and told him not to let anyone see what was in it. When all of the kids began chasing him, I went into the classroom and put the pistol and shells in my desk. We had the kind of desks on which the lid lifts, and our things were kept underneath the writing surface.

The bell rang and I wondered how and when I'd get the chance to shoot Miss Halsey. It made me feel in charge. As she entered, I decided to pull the trigger when she got only one or two seats away, so I'd be sure not to miss.

As Miss Halsey moved about the room busily, I thought about the way she shook when she laughed. Why hadn't she believed me? I sort of liked my teacher—but it was her fault, so I had to kill her.

Meanwhile, Aunt Fay had checked on her pistol again and,

finding it gone, had phoned the police. Since I had inquired about it that morning, the schoolroom was the first place they came to look. When the officers and the principal entered, Miss Halsey was halfway between them and my seat.

"Excuse us, Ma'am, we'd like to speak to Jim Tucker, Fay Kane's boy." Immediately I wanted to run. Cops had always meant real trouble to me. Instead, I reached into my desk and took out the cocked gun. As I quickly threw it at the officers, the pistol hit the floor and fired. Miss Halsey screamed, then fell to the floor. I hadn't even aimed it, and she was dying—or dead. Kids gasped, some screamed.

The principal and policemen stooped to help her, and I ran out the side door into the arms of a waiting officer.

The patrolmen clamped the first set of handcuffs on my wrists and easily threw me into the back seat of the police car. Both officers got into the front seat, not thinking that a boy of nine could cause much trouble.

They headed for Kern County Jail, talking on the way. The handcuffs were loose on my wrists, so I worked my hands until they were free. Then I tapped one policeman on the shoulder. "Want these back? I don't need 'em." For once I wasn't trying to act smart. They didn't see it that way, and from then on, whenever I was taken into custody, the police not only cuffed but chained and shackled me to make sure I couldn't get loose.

At the station, I was put into a cell. Alone. Broken. Afraid. And all there knew it. Aunt Fay was called, but she didn't come. The officers encouraged my fears at first, jeering, "Well, well, so now Kern County has its own Billy the Kid! How about that? Come and see this brave little killer. Ain't he somethin'? Only nine; so he'll be the youngest one we ever hanged. Had a real pretty pistol, too, to use on his teacher. Look at this little beauty! Stole it from his own mother that took him in."

They spoke to each other and to me as though I were a lost cause. "Had it so good with his new home but didn't appreciate it." I believed a lot of what was said, but knowing that Aunt Fay had taken me for herself, not for my benefit, I began to hate her, too.

I was overcome with terror as I visualized Miss Halsey dead. I hadn't really hated her and wished I hadn't killed her. Why hadn't she believed me when I told her I didn't shoot that paper wad? If only people would listen to me. I didn't deserve to die! The school was at fault, too. How I hated that P.E. teacher and the principal. They also thought I'd lied.

My suffering went on and on, while the officers on duty knew that Miss Halsey had only fainted when the gun fired and the bullet had gone into the ceiling. When mealtime came, I didn't dare eat. I was a criminal, ready for the gallows. I'd seen enough TV to know that! The next meal would be my last; after that I'd be hanged.

I began to plead for my life; I'd work, I'd be good, I'd never again do anything wrong. Even in school, I promised to behave. I meant every word, too. But their game went on.

After a few hours, the officers took me to Juvenile Hall, but I wouldn't eat there, either. They finally told me that my teacher had only fainted, but I refused to believe it until she came to see me. I could hardly believe my eyes. She spoke softly, "Eat, Jim. I only fainted. The officers have told me how sorry you are. You have so many problems for a child, I hope someday, somehow, you'll get help."

I nodded as she went on. "What's going to become of you, Jim? You're bright, but such a problem." She looked sorry for me and started to leave.

Tears were in my eyes. "I'm glad you're okay, Miss Halsey. And I really didn't shoot that paper wad." She shook her head and kept on walking.

Aunt Fay never wanted to see me again, for I'd been too much trouble for an old lady who was trying to be kind. The adoption was annulled at her request, and the judge ordered me to reform school.

There I continued to act tough—for the sake of survival. This time I was in custody for about two years. As a loner, I didn't get into much trouble and soon became used to the correctional system.

By age eleven I was as big as many men and bigger than some. In a one-to-one fight I'd always win, and some of the fellows vowed to get even. One day while I was in a room with no counselor on the floor, a gang surrounded me. "On yer hands and knees, Tucker," they sneered.

"Oh yeah? Says who?" I spit and took on the whole group. But they got the best of me. While some held me down, others punched again and again until my wind was knocked out and I collapsed.

The guys pulled off my pants, and it was like Juvenile Hall again. Filled with hatred and anger, I determined never to let it happen again. I would escape and find refuge with Katie.

The next day I started a fight in the yard, and before anyone could be sure who'd done it, I broke away, jumped the fence and ran. The wind on my face felt good. By using back roads and being careful, I avoided being caught. Older and wiser now, I headed for Bakersfield and Katie's little home. Lucky at hitchhiking, I knew how to get there without being seen in the Cottonwood area of Aunt Fay's.

Sure enough, Katie's door was unlocked. It was good to be there, alone and safe. Exhausted, I fell asleep on her bed, my large shoes on the floor.

A blanket had been thrown over me as I slept, and when I

awoke the smell of something delicious was coming from the kitchen. Katie hummed softly what I believed to be a hymn. Strange how this short black lady's singing made me think of the garden my mother used to sing about. Walking into her kitchen, it felt natural to say, "Hi! I remembered what you said about your door, so I came back."

"I always knowed you would when you had to rest or needed a friend." She smiled and went on working over the shiny black stove.

"I can't stay long. You'll be in trouble if I do." She didn't answer, but nodded.

"Well, you growed a lot, Jim Tuckah! Now, you gonna eat like a man! We got ham hocks 'n beans, an' good cornbread."

It was food fit for a king. I stuffed myself, then we sat in her kitchen in the light of the oil lamp and talked.

"Katie ain't askin' you no questions. But Katie's gonna tell you some things. Chile, I heard what they said you done, about the teachah, and the gun an' all. I thank my Jesus you don' hurt her. But I thank my Jesus more that you now outta that wicked-spirit home. Ol' Miz Kane, she cain't he'p herself, but you got out jus' in time! Maybe you don' dress so fancy no more, maybe lots of things. You jus' remembah, friend Katie don' lie, and she know about these things. God shows me things, Jim. Go almost any place an' be bettah off. Even jail, an' that's the truth!"

"I guess so."

Katie talked about things I didn't understand, but I believed her. She was good and kind, someone to look up to. Full and tired, I just wanted to rest and not have to think.

Katie got up first. "Now, before we rest, come an' see what I got. I figgered maybe some day that Tuckah chile be back, an' he need clothes. I got 'em. They jus' right, too!" she clucked.

Sure enough, Katie had some good, used clothing which fit

me. Not fancy, but clean. It was a pleasure to bathe and put them on. I took my time; the water nearly put me to sleep after her good dinner.

"Tonight I'll sleep on the couch," she insisted later. "You need a good rest. I know you go far away, and I wisht I could keep you. They wouldn' let no ol' black lady take you in."

"I'll be just fine on my own," I reassured.

"Tomorrow we have a good breakfas' an' you slip out early. Don' fergit the lunch I'll pack and leave out for you."

Katie awakened me when my breakfast was ready, then went to work early in someone's home. Before leaving, I looked around the house. It was so neat I had to go back and make the bed. Before walking out the door, I picked up a scrap of paper from the dresser and wrote, "Thank you, Ma'am. Yours truly, Jim." I placed the note on her old Bible, grabbed the lunch and left, taking also a happy memory.

As soon as I could safely leave the back roads and get onto a main highway, I began to thumb a ride. The pickup took me to Los Angeles, which is where I was headed. In detention I'd heard of a place there where a person could get lost in the crowd.

I lied about my name and age, telling the people that I was sixteen, so my parents thought I was old enough to travel alone. Convinced that my Uncle Jake was waiting for me, they let me out downtown. Before long, I found my way to Pershing Square, the place I'd heard about from older boys where everything happened. It was worse than they'd said. I walked around trying not to stare, acting like I knew the score. This was a hangout for winos, homosexuals, pimps, hustlers or hookers, and every kind of criminal or pervert. I intended only to drink a little and buy a few street drugs, as the place made me very uneasy.

Sitting by a bush, I kept my eye on those around me. Everyone seemed totally at ease. No longer able to hold my eyes open, I laid back and looked up at the sky, then dozed. It was getting cool and I longed for a warmer jacket or, better yet, a place indoors to sleep. My food had been gone a long time.

The next thing I knew, two men—probably in their thirties—were sitting on each side of me. Hearing their voices, I sat up.

"You're new around, right?"

"Yeah."

"Goin' home tonight?"

"Nah."

"You a runaway?"

"Maybe."

"Wanta sleep at our place?"

"Why should I?"

"We like to help kids out. It's gettin' cold. C'mon, it's okay. Our place is better than the park."

Pretending not to care, I roze lazily to my feet. We strode several blocks to an old building and into a rather nice apartment. It was good to be indoors, and they *did* have a bed and a couch.

"You wanta sleep in the middle or on the couch?" They both laughed.

"I want something to eat," I mumbled.

One giggled like some of the older girls I'd had down in my cave. "That's my job, honey." Sure enough, he quickly set some food on the table for us. The other one put on his slippers, lit his pipe and turned on some music.

It all seemed crazy. The one with the giggle soon left the table and cooed, "I'm gonna slip into something more comfortable, dear." Off came his street clothes and on went a long, colorful robe with nothing under.

When we finished eating, the one with the pipe got some wine, and we went to sit in the couch area. He sat in a chair, and the giggler sprawled by his partner on the arm of the chair.

"Got any of the good junk left?"

"You'd better believe it."

"Put on your robe, and let's have at it."

The robe was laid out for him and he put it on, then using the needle the giggler got his first. He was relaxing on their bed when the second one had his fix. I'd never seen the needle used before, but had heard a lot about it. They both were so relaxed and happy on the bed, they invited me to come and lay in the middle.

"You mean lie, dear," said the sissy one. "Huh-uh, let's lay him." More laughter.

Soon the one acting like the man said to me, "You're all tensed up. Wanta relax like us?"

"Could try it, I guess, but I never used a needle before." He gave it to me himself, then hid everything. In a moment of joypopping, I relaxed. My whole body felt loose, floating, easy. Nothing seemed to matter. My worries disappeared. It was a wonderful release from the past, the hurt, and I was happy.

"Hey, this is all right! Gimme some more."

"Later," the one that acted like the man said. "Just take it slow and easy; rest now." I don't think I ever did end up in the middle.

After a few rustling sounds from under their blanket, and talk—"Tomorrow I'll get you . . . tomorrow we'll enjoy"—they soon dozed.

Tomorrow came and all three of us had a big letdown, and the wonderful expectancy of their day was gone. After they nodded off again, I stole some things from them which I could sell, then left.

Early morning found me back on the streets selling the stolen items. While loitering in Pershing Square, I was approached by an older man, also homosexual. He held out fifty dollars to entice me to his home. Needing the money, I went willingly. He treated me kindly and was honest about his request. Not interested in a regular relationship, I took the money and left. The cash was more than enough for clothing, shoes, and food. There was plenty left for some relaxing whites and reds. The pusher who supplied the drugs told me how to earn more cash. (He already knew I'd earned the fifty.) Out of the need to survive, I decided to continue selling my body.

My appetite grew with my body; I was always hungry for food or for drugs and alcohol. At one low point, I spent all of my money on drugs and ate from the trash can behind a big market where they tossed wilted vegetables. Soon afterward, I overdosed on a hallucinogenic drug and was picked up for disturbing the peace, drug use and vagrancy.

I passed my thirteenth birthday at Fred C. Nellis Reform School in Whittier, California. In time I was transferred to Khaki Boys' Ranch for being so uncooperative at the school.

The outdoor life was good for me, and the food seemed better than at other institutions. I even had a pet donkey; it was mine for as long as I was there, and his care was to be my total responsibility. I named him Elmer after a cartoon character. We spent a lot of free time together at the corral.

At this institution, as with the others, I didn't have to look for the group of boys I knew from previous sentences. Many were there ahead of me. I turned fourteen at Khaki, and during that year, it was announced that there was to be, of all things, a donkey barbecue for the public. There had been meat rationing in our country during World War II, and people stood in line to buy horsemeat legally. I suppose a donkey barbecue wasn't so strange, but at the time I laughed with the other boys about it.

The kid who sold the most tickets to the event would win the brand new red-and-chrome Schwinn bicycle on display at the ranch. We were driven to various places to sell tickets and I was careful to say "Please" and "Thank you." When the final count was in, I'd won the bike, fair and square! It was to be awarded to me publicly at the barbecue the next weekend.

We boys were busy with the preparations until late Friday evening. I helped rake and clean the area, and to put up tables which we made by placing planks over sawhorses. Folding chairs and benches were brought out, and pits were dug. By bedtime all was in order for the spectacular event.

Some of the boys helped the cooks, and we saw cake, pies, and rolls being baked. They boiled huge pans of potatoes and eggs for potato salad, and prepared big kettles of beans for baking at the crack of dawn.

With all the excitement, I was as wide awake as an owl, even though I'd worked hard and was tired. Since I was happier on a day-to-day basis, pills no longer had their hold on my body. Adjusting to the thought of never having a real home, I determined to make the best of my situation. The honor system wasn't too hard to live with. If we did our chores, we had free time for movies and games, and I had Elmer. Now I'd have a new bike, too. The feeling of having won something fairly was good, too.

Few chores were assigned to us the day of the barbecue. When I awakened rather late, the delicious smell of barbecued meat filled the air. People had arrived and, as I looked out, I could see them being served. I hurriedly dressed, making sure to look neat when I stepped up to claim the bike. Instead of sitting down, I took my piled-high plate to the corral to feed Elmer and eat. Suddenly, I froze. The hide of my pet donkey was draped over the fence to dry in the sun. In disbelief and horror, I threw the plate of food into his stall and ran for the hills. I retched and spit until I could vomit no more. My eyes watered, and my body was wet with sweat and tears.

When the churning inside me stopped, I took out again on a run. The faster I could get away, the better. The bike was no longer of importance. Why *my* donkey? Why hadn't anyone asked me? I couldn't believe that I'd sold the most tickets to get people to eat my pet.

In time I fell to the floor in an old abandoned shack in the seclusion that surrounded the ranch. I'd be missed when my name was called to accept the bike, but more running was out of the question. Exhausted, I stayed in the shack the rest of that day and all night. In the morning I made my way to the highway, hoping to hitch a ride to Katie's, but was picked up by a patrol car instead.

Evidently the officers believed me when I explained why I had run. They took me to Juvenile Hall, where I was released within a few weeks into what was to have been a good foster home.

I had a chance to visit Katie while at my next placement, but she was gone. The people who now lived in her little house had known of her, but she had died.

Just knowing that she wasn't there made the world a lonelier place for me after that.

Chapter 10
CAUGHT IN THE ACT

Reverend Hugh Fry and his wife, Jeanne, agreed to give me a foster home. They were licensed and said I deserved another chance.

I liked this couple. They seemed interested in me. I'd have to go to church since Hugh was a preacher, but they were polite and cordial, using endearing terms to each other. Possibly nearing middle age, they were neatly dressed. She was small and attractive, but didn't wear a speck of makeup. At fifteen I knew a bit of color was in style and would make this lady even prettier. But Reverend Fry wouldn't allow it. He was slightly balding and had a potbelly, making the pair seem mismatched.

During the months I was with them, Jeanne jumped to satisfy her husband's every need. "Find my blue shirt, my tie and socks to match." He appeared to appreciate and love her, and she seemed glad to hear his rewarding words, "Thank you, dear."

She cooked what he told her to prepare, kept their home neat as a pin, was kind to those who came or phoned, and I decided to be like Hugh Fry. He was boss. I couldn't think of a better setup.

They insisted that I attend church whenever the doors were open, and I didn't cause trouble for myself by resisting. Living with a minister was a good cover, and my benefits were too good—drinking, street drugs, and a chance to do a few easy, small thefts. All on the sly, of course. I could easily pick the P.E. locks at school and find things to sell. Sometimes even money. I also stole from the girls' purses now and then.

A man who said he was a doctor traded me pills for the goods I stole. I operated alone, and none of my contacts realized where I lived.

I was careful to pop pills only when alone at the Frys'. It was important not to let the Reverend catch me at anything wrong, as he talked continually of sin. He was a screamer in church: "Repent, you sinners!" And once in a weak moment, I almost did. He yelled loud and clear about burning in Hell forever, and that voice and description sent a chill down my spine and over the entire church. Some of the same people always repented. He could scare *them*, but not me. I hated cowards. I was too tough to fall for that, and enough of a con to suspect he was one of another kind.

The altar would be lined mostly with women, a few old men, and some boys and girls. He'd make them kneel and confess their sins. Then he'd pray something like this:

"Oh, sister, repent in the name of the Lord! God, forgive this stubborn woman. Help her to be willing to clean up after her drunken husband and not complain. He may beat her and bruise her, but even if he kills her, she'll be with You in eternity. . . ."

". . . Lord, You know this young girl got carried away in her boyfriend's car, so forgive her and as soon as she can see him, make her bring him to church to repent also. . . ."

". . . God, here we have a man who doesn't know how to bring his wife and children into submission. Cause him to whip them if they won't mind and understand that You said he's the boss. . . ." Then he'd add something like, "Go home tonight and shape them up, brother."

". . . Now, Lord, here's a young man in his tender teens. He's got to keep the right friends. You forgive him, God. He didn't understand that wanton Jezebels are out there in Your land today, just a-waitin' to trap him!"

On and on he'd go, making the repenting time a gossip session, and favoring the things he did to Jeanne that seemed wrong to me.

The way he got money and things from the people bothered me, too. He'd tell them how much to bring, such as, "God said to give the biggest bill you have in your wallet, Brother John. You trust the Lord, and He'll bring it back tenfold." When Brother John would admit he only had some change, Reverend Fry would say, "God don't care; He'll take that nice wrist watch. Jewelry is of the devil, anyhow."

Once he said, "God spoke to me just before I came onto the platform. You all take your gold and your silver—yes, earrings and jewelry. Pass the basket, you ushers, and woe unto you who don't obey when the prophet of the Lord speaks to you."

Sure enough, off came a lot of jewelry for the collection plate. It seemed unfair, but if the people were so stupid as to let him con them, it was their problem. At home he pawed through the items and admired them. It reminded me of Aunt Fay's powers to make people fork over their money. My method of stealing seemed easier. I could just take what I wanted whenever the need arose. What Reverend Fry did with the take was a mystery to me. I remembered the sadness on the faces of the people who had given up their possessions. Did God want us to be sad? If He did, I'd had my share.

One day while Jeanne was gone a few hours, I had some questions about my chores at the house. I ran next door to the church and pushed open the door of the office, intending to ask quickly and hurry back to my work. "Only me, for a quick question," I announced cheerfully as the door opened wide.

Two voices hollered at the same time, "Get out!" and "Oh, no!" There upon the lovely carpet was the minister in a naked and intimate embrace with the wife of a friend at the church. Shocked and disgusted, I decided to get out of the house before Jeanne came home.

In my room, I gathered all my pills into one sack and took off with only my jacket. I never looked back.

After sleeping in a strange church that night, I hit the road toward the country. One farm wife gave me lunch but said she had no work to offer. At another place, I lied about my age and asked for work, but was called names and told they didn't want any strangers around. Unable to find a job, I headed back to town where I shoplifted some food and spent a few foggy days on uppers and downers.

Soon I was picked up as a runaway again. Reverend Fry had told the police that I'd left for no good reason, and I let their story stand out of respect for Jeanne and chose Juvenile Hall.

In private Reverend Fry apologized for what I'd seen. "It'll never happen again. I'm not a bad man, just human. I'm sorry for hurting your faith. Can you forgive me enough to keep quiet about what you saw?"

My honesty seemed to shock him. "Yeah, I'll keep quiet . . . for Jeanne. But you don't deserve her."

For once that loudmouth didn't point a finger or say a word. About a year or two later, between times in and out of reform schools or jail, I slipped in where he was preaching to quite a crowd. He looked much older, and he was quieter and gentle with the people. I sensed a new sincerity about him. This man now believed what he was saying—I feel certain of it—and I was glad for him.

Never for a moment did I buy any of the Jesus stuff, but I still was glad for Jeanne. She sat in the front, very well dressed and with just the right amount of makeup. The Reverend had done his own repenting along the way. At least he wasn't trying to rip the people off any more.

Chapter 11
HOME "SWEET" HOME

For the vagrancy and drug charges after leaving the Frys, I was sent to Preston, a good-sized facility of the California Youth Authority System. Perhaps the court felt a change of scenery would be good for me, as Preston is in northern California, around Ione.

During my time on the streets, I'd used something to keep me from coming unglued, to pick me up, or take me down. After a few days in Preston, I was able to get bennies, whites, red devils, even rainbows. With drug desires and ideas on how to get them swirling in my brain, I strode into the exercise area one day and stopped short. There across the yard hobbled a boy on crutches. This kid was small and appeared somewhat like Jackie would look now. Cautiously, I strolled toward him, then caught my breath. It *was* Jackie! Paying no attention to anyone or anything, he looked so dark and skinny. And tired. He wore braces on both legs with a thick leather belt to hold them in line. Watching him, I wondered what to do or say, then decided to approach. Suddenly, he recognized me, too, but showed little emotion. I wanted to at least shake hands. Having not seen each other in years, we should have been overjoyed at the reunion. But he didn't reach out to take my extended hand.

"Jim, you S.O.B.! So . . . my big brother's in here, too!" He laughed like he was glad, and that rubbed me the wrong way.

Jackie was in for theft. I soon discovered that he cussed more than just about anyone. Seldom did I feel the need to swear as he did, even as I got older.

We swapped stories for some time that day. Jackie was an addict also, except he got his drugs legally by pretending to the authorities that he was in pain. Jackie was so different it hurt. He was mean and bitter, especially toward me. Perhaps it was part of his act.

We saw each other for a couple of minutes each day for about a week. "Mother is coming to take me home," he blurted one morning. This stunned me, for I hadn't heard from her since that visit in the Bakersfield Juvenile Hall. "I'll tell her you're here; maybe now you can visit with her." It sounded like sarcasm, and the fact that she'd kept in touch with him all along made me feel even more rejected.

"I have . . .no . . . mother!" My voice revealed all the anger and bitterness that had been bottled up for years.

Without warning, Jackie struck me alongside my ear with his crutch. A cruel look darkened his face, making me forget that he was the brother I'd always wanted to protect. I shoved and knocked him down. Had he not been a cripple, he would have felt the full force of my pounding fist. Instead I held myself in check. Already in trouble with the authorities for hitting him, I just stood looking down on him until the guards escorted me into solitary.

In that lonely cell, I was sick from drug withdrawal and the shattered dreams of a reunited family. I'd wanted Jackie to have a good life, had hoped that he was off in a good school and hoped we'd meet again on good terms. I'd truly believed that we would always be close. Now, with both of us changed, the future seemed hopeless.

I was wrong. Just before my release a few weeks later, the court contacted my mother. With no foster home available, she agreed to see me again. Mama had remarried, and her husband told the authorities that he could and would control me.

When I rejoined Mama and Jackie, it wasn't at all as I had imagined. Plastic surgery had surely helped, but her disfigured face was a constant reminder of the attack. Still, I hoped we could somehow pick up the pieces and find happiness. Perhaps with this new start a way could be found to make up for our lost years. It was good that Mama had a husband; she had needed someone when I wasn't there. John was loving and considerate of her, but it was soon evident that he felt little, if anything, for me. I was in no way prepared for the conflicts which would come my way.

Mama was pregnant, and I was surprised to see other small children in their home. "These are your three little brothers and sisters, and you're going to have to take care of them, Jim," John announced. "Your mother can't now, and I have to work." The kids crowded around me, and I liked them. Still, small children were something to get used to.

The court had told Mama and John all about me. She was quiet about my record, but John took a totally different attitude. He dug up every rotten thing I'd ever done, making much of knowing that I'd hung around with perverts. "I'll be watching you, Jim. Better know this right now. I can whip you good 'n proper, so you'd better stay straight."

I resented him for throwing the past in my face. What did he know about survival? He and Mama had been married a long time by the looks of their children, but he hadn't tried to help me. Since no one else had wanted to take me in, he'd agreed. And this made me feel even more uncomfortable.

Because he worked with a road construction gang each day, I

did my best not to make trouble. I cooked some, got the younger ones up and did housework and yardwork, trying to cooperate. I had hardly any access to pills and was managing that fairly well, too. At times Jackie and I were quarrelsome and nervous, but this was common for kids not long out of lockup. Often we were like brothers should be, but usually Jackie was too much out of it from his medication to be fun.

Mama kept to her bed most of the time, and it was a great disappointment to both Jackie and me to see her pop pills and drink wine. We were old enough to know that this was not good for a pregnant woman. Now and then she'd say she was glad we were all together again and that things would be much better for all of us when the baby was born and she was up and looking after her family again.

Since her husband was earning our living, I respected him and wished we could get along. But he found fault with everything I did. Maybe he was tired and couldn't handle his own frustration. Still, I was getting the dirty end of it again. Especially that night in the basement. I took a load of wood down which I'd just chopped, and John began to call me names. The worst he could think of.

"You're no good and you never will be!" he ended his tirade. My anger was rising but I realized he'd been drinking and turned to leave.

"You stand there and hear me, or you'll wish you had." He stormed toward me with his fist doubled. In a blaze of cursing, he called me a sissy and a mama's boy.

"Do you want me to leave and live somewhere else?" I was mad and started up the steps.

He quickly calmed down and became pleasant. "Oh, come on over here, Jim. Don't leave me down here alone." He was a big man, and I was afraid of him. "C'mon, be friendly. Have a drink." Cautiously, I sat on the floor near him and took the bottle from his extended hand.

Mama was about due to deliver their baby. Maybe it was anxiety that was causing him to act up. I was glad for the wine and kept exchanging drinks from the bottle with him. I ignored or replied and let him ramble on, as I got drunk myself. It seemed a long time since I'd relaxed. Suddenly, John lunged toward me and clapped his hand over my mouth, warning me what would happen if I made a noise. Too drunk to fight him off, I was molested by my stepfather. My hatred for him burned as he forced himself on me.

"Don't go whining to your mother; she'd never believe you," he panted as I ran up the stairs and outside. He was right. She wouldn't. "The court told us all the stuff you done, sissy!"

Would I ever be free of the past? Did it have to hound me in the home of my own mother? Wasn't it enough that I'd fought hard to lick the bad dreams, even cut way down on the drugs that it took for me to survive? By then I was quite sober and feeling sick to my stomach and at heart. Leaving home would mean reform school again, something I didn't want at this time. I avoided John after that.

Months after the baby's birth, Mama still depended on me to help in the house. I could count on her calls for help, Jackie griping at me, and John's sharp criticisms. The little kids were pleasant, even appreciative, but I was fed up. It was time to split—but how and when?

John caught Jackie and me smoking together. Although he smoked tobacco, it was wrong for us. In his anger he made us sit at the table in the kitchen and each light a cigarette. We were then made to smoke until it began to burn our lips. "Chew it up. . . . Now, swallow it with this! You want to be grown-up and drink wine? Here . . . have some!"

We took the glasses and drank. Both of us got very sick, especially Jackie. It could have killed him. John knew of his heavy medication, but the cruelty never left his eyes. Jackie looked as though he were going to pass out as he hobbled on his crutches out the back door, only to fall on his face in the dirt and vomit.

As I fixed breakfast for the little ones the next morning, I decided to have it out with my stepfather.

"John, we've got to talk. Maybe we were wrong to smoke, but you didn't do right last night. Jackie is still sick, and he can't take it like I can. Make our mother get off the stuff and do some of the work. We all need a mother around here."

"Look, kid," he fumed, "in my house you do as I say. I call the shots here, and don't you ever forget it!"

"I'm right, and you know it!" I sassed. "You and Mama get straight, and maybe we can try then. Get her out of bed, and make her a fulltime Mom. I'm tired of being your housekeeper!"

In one swift movement John grabbed and shoved me to the basement door and down the steps. He tied me to some old bed springs with clothesline rope and began to whip me with an ironing cord. As he laid it on, he cursed and threatened to leave me there.

"Argue with me, will ya? Tell *me* how to run my own home, will ya? You're a loser! A sweet old lady couldn't change you, even when she gave you everything her money could afford. A preacher couldn't even make you do right. *I'll* beat some sense into that thick head of yours! Cry, you sissy, cry! You ain't too tough to cry!"

I'd have died first. John would never see me cry. A while later he returned to untie me. "Well, let's see how long it is before I get to do this again. Now git!"

I ran outdoors, determined to "git" as far away as possible. Forever.

I was in the yard alone and hurting, inside and out, when Jackie hobbled over to me, cussing and griping. "You look like you want to be out of it, but don't go lookin' for my good stuff; I need it myself."

"Knock it off. I just had a fight with John!"

"You probably asked for it," he sneered, continuing to work on me with mean, nasty digs. I blew my stack, and Jackie took off as fast as his crutches would take him. I reached down, picked up a big can and threw it. The can split his head, and he fell. Jackie yelled, and some of the little kids came running, then went back in to get John. The time had come for me to split. Jackie's cuss words were the last thing I heard as I took off running.

Chapter 12
I ALONE SURVIVED

I hit the road without baggage or money and with no sense of direction. With my thumb signaling for a ride, I just wanted to get away.

"Hi! Hop in, handsome! Whereya headin'?"

I stared at the gorgeous creature who'd stopped to give me a lift. "Oh, I dunno. A change of scenery somewhere. Where you goin'?"

It wouldn't sound too cool to tell her I'd just had a beating and was running away from home.

"New Orleans. Ever been there?"

"No, not yet. I always did want to see that town, though," I lied. The con in me was rising to action. Maybe she would take me with her if I played it right.

"Well, I'll have to work my way there, but I'll make it in a few days, and it'll be worth it to get home."

Her plans included a stop in Los Angeles. Her smile and look of confidence helped me feel secure.

"What's your name, honey? How old are you?"

"Jim—and I'm eighteen. What's yours?"

"Arlene. That suit you, honey?"

"Sure!" I continued to size her up. Sensing it, she tossed her long, dark hair over her shoulder and took turns looking at me and the road. Arlene's brown eyes seemed to blend with her warm smile. Long eyelashes lay against her olive complexion, and her makeup looked maybe a bit too heavy, but it suited her. I liked everything about this lady, including her long, beautifully polished fingernails and pretty, colorful dress. Painted toenails matched the polish on her fingernails as they peeked from her sandals.

After riding in silence awhile, broken only by bits of small talk, we came to a lonely spot along the highway. Arlene pulled off the road, stopped, then turned off the engine. "Tell me, Jim, you ever had a woman?"

"Sure," I lied again because all I had had were the girls in the cave. I'd heard plenty about the kind of sex she meant from guys on the inside and some on the outside.

"Would you like me?" She spoke softly, her eyes beckoning as she looked me over. It all seemed so right and good.

"Yes."

She kissed me, at first gently, then again hard. I responded to her every movement. She encouraged me by pressing close, then closer. In a quick movement that I learned later was performed among those in the oldest profession in the world, her body was bare and we were melted together in the seat of her car. She took her time, and I thought it was beautiful. Much later I learned that she knew I was not eighteen, and that she was my first "real" woman. Arlene seemed pleased at both. To a frustrated kid with a sore back from a beating, holding Arlene close was a healing balm.

Leaning back against the seat, I rested my head near hers, my mind and body free of tension. I realized her trade but didn't care. For me life was moment-to-moment, and at this moment I was contented.

"Will you travel all the way with me, Jim?" she asked after a long silence.

"Maybe," I teased. She couldn't have driven me off with a stick.

"I'd like to have you be my little brother. I need you."

"Little brother? Me? Why me?"

"Well, you're the kinda guy a woman needs sometimes. No strings attached. We could help each other—in lots of ways. You need a place to live and a way to live. Right?" She had me all figured out.

No strings attached was what I wanted. "You got a deal," I grinned. She hugged me. "But I got no money, not even clothes except what I'm wearin'."

"Yeah, but we both got ways, so we'll get the money. And honey, I've already got the clothes for you. You'll see! We'll have us a time."

Arlene had enough money for food and for a room at a cheap motel. Once in our room, I was in for a surprise. She had three suitcases full of men's clothing! They fit me—all six feet, one hundred seventy pounds of me. I heard myself laughing aloud. What a lucky break! Broke and miserable in the morning, I was now alone with a beautiful woman who'd just furnished me, Jim Tucker, with the fanciest wardrobe I'd ever seen. When I tried the clothes on, I wanted to strut—which I did, just for her! "Wow! Thanks, Sis."

"See, I was right. You're sharp. Together we'll go places. But before we can, we've got to get some gasoline. Can't use our money for that."

"You've got a gas can, of course?" I asked, still laughing.

"Sho' nuf, honey! I'd better practice my New Orleans talk, too!"

Between stealing gas (her Oklahoma credit card), buying food and cheap lodging, we made it to New Orleans. You can hear music and see interesting people at all hours in that city, and the odor of the creole food lingered everywhere.

We stopped in an area with huge, old ornamental-trimmed homes surrounded by walls and gardens. When I was introduced to a pleasant group of women as Arlene's little brother, they all laughed and welcomed me.

I was among a group of prostitutes of all ages and descriptions who soon were speculating on where I might like to go to see the sights. For a few weeks I accepted their hospitality and had the run of the house—and, with Arlene's permission, the love of these ladies. Then Arlene revealed her true motive for taking me on.

"They really do love you, Jim," she spoke of the other women. "They want you for their little brother, too. We share everything here. Listen, you know the score. You been out and around, and you know the area some now. You could make some good contacts to bring us men, and you're big enough to handle anyone who gets out of line. You've played it right, now we want you for the honeyman!"

My face registered shock. "You've been sweet and they like that," she continued. "I'll help you learn, and we'll manage the whole group. You'll get a percentage of everything so you can live easy! Get your own apartment, if you need to be alone."

"I'm no pimp, Arlene! No bunch of women's gonna keep me!"

"You'll learn. Please, Jim, give it a try. What can you lose?"

The whole deal made me feel disloyal. These were my friends. How could I be the one to bring in the men, even for a percentage of the earnings? It was time to hit the road again, only now I was sorry. It was hard to tell Arlene, but I couldn't skip without saying goodbye. I managed to let all of them know of my appreciation for their offer by a clumsy short speech about how I admired them too much.

They hugged me and Arlene said, "It's okay, honey. This racket isn't for everyone. You've been fun and sweet, more of a man than a lot we've had who are older."

Then she made one last cunning effort to hold me. "You don't have to leave just because you turned us down." But I insisted on leaving, and the women took up a collection so that I wouldn't have to travel broke. I accepted that and one suitcase of the clothes and took off running, not daring to look back at my friends.

I'd told Arlene I was going to Oklahoma to look up some friends, but changed my mind and headed back to Los Angeles. My thumb out for a ride, I grinned, *Yeah! Now for sure, I am a man.*

Back in the familiar L.A. area—better dressed than before and somewhat wiser and a bit older—I lied about my age and hung around some honky-tonks. I enjoyed my completely undisciplined life for a while, but the money soon ran out. Craftily, I planned how to replenish my loot.

Slightly drunk one evening, I was propositioned by a woman in a bar and went home with her. She wasn't at all like the women I'd recently been with. Her obscene talk and ill-mannered ways bothered me. When she wasn't looking, I lifted a few pieces of her jewelry and split. She called the police, and I was picked up with the goods still on me. Apparently afraid of the publicity, she didn't press charges. Nevertheless the police held me on a vagrancy charge.

John and Mama didn't want me back, which suited me just fine. I was given a choice between two "addresses." The first was the big boys' reform school in Lancaster.

"You've been in and out of trouble since you were seven! The file on you is thick. You don't deserve a tough place like that, but we want you off the streets while you're growing up."

"What's the other choice?" I murmured.

"Think you're quite a man, don't you? All right. We'll give you a chance to be a man, a *real* man. Your last opportunity, Tucker—join the service and help your country."

Some choice. I hated discipline of any kind. Least of all what was dished out inside. To escape the things I didn't like, at age sixteen and one half I was accepted into the U.S. Marine Corps, where they were given the tough job of making a man of me.

Before I could go into the armed forces, a waiver of the age requirement had to be signed. I suppose the court or my mother did that. At five one morning a Marine sergeant escorted me to the train at the L.A. depot where we joined another group of guys. When we reached San Diego, we were met by another sergeant, a short, snappy-type, skinny guy who yelled everything he said.

"Put your stuff at your feet! Stand up straight! Put your thumbs at the seams of your trousers! Now, don't move!"

We didn't. Another sergeant stood in front of us in a few minutes, while the other two processed our paperwork. The sergeant was a big, bulldog-looking Marine, and I hated him for the way he strutted. Parading up and down in front of us, he screamed insults about our looks, deliberately inciting a fighting spirit in us. Mine rose fast. He stopped shouting long enough to stand in front of me, staring as though I were obnoxious. His next words were just what it took to thrust me into action.

"If anyone in this bad lookin' bunch thinks they're big, and bad, and tough—tough enough to step out here and take me on . . . jump out and do it!"

I leaped from the line and knocked him cold.

The other Marines grabbed and held me until the Shore

Patrol arrived. They put me in the brig for a few days to cool off.

It took just that much confinement to make me decide against the Corps. As soon as they let me out, I went A.W.O.L. (absent without leave). On the streets again, I soon met and fell in love with a pretty girl named Jane, all of sixteen like me. She thought I was nineteen. We saw each other as often as possible, but her parents were strict and wealthy, and she wasn't allowed out nearly as much as I wanted to see her. Jane had me in such a spin that I didn't care about much else.

We would arrange for Hilda, her girlfriend, to invite her out, then she and I would meet. In love, as we understood it then, we decided to get married. I was living without a job, depending on petty thefts for support. I had to find a way to do better.

Hilda was poor and lived in a foster home. I believed her when she told Jane and me that her foster father had tried to molest her. We decided to go to Mexico and get married—the three of us. I'd marry Jane because I loved her. She'd be my real wife. And I'd marry Hilda to get her away from the home. We would all live together, happily.

The next day Jane withdrew her savings account of six hundred dollars and hocked some expensive jewelry. Hilda had a few dollars, and I had stolen about seventy-five bucks from a liquor store.

In Tijuana we found a place that handled quick marriages, signed some papers and stood before a man who spoke no English. But in a rather nice ceremony, he pronounced Jane and me husband and wife. Soon we were on our honeymoon. Hilda made herself scarce for a day; then I kept my promise to marry her also, and we all went on a honeymoon!

Back in San Diego the fun soon came to an end. The three of us were taken into custody one day as we sat in a restaurant.

The Marine Corps had filed a list of charges against me and so had the state government. The Marines were there first, charging desertion. The state had a longer list, including contributing to the delinquency of minors, kidnapping two juveniles and causing them to leave the country, and theft (Jane's money and jewelry).

To complicate matters, I learned that Jane's father was a Marine Corps captain, a man with considerable influence. He quickly had the two Mexican marriages annulled, and it was only to protect his daughter that he agreed to drop all charges against me. Hilda's parents did also. Incredibly, the matter was quickly settled during one brief appearance by all of us in federal court. The state charges were dropped, and I was given a general court-martial.

The girls blew me a kiss as they left, and almost immediately a Marine Shore Patrol barked, "C'mon, Romeo; that'll have to do you for a while."

Jane's father had been assured that I'd do eighteen months at Federal Island, also known as Yerba Buena. I also received a dishonorable discharge from the Corps.

In the brig I had time to let bitter feelings further harden my heart. Life had dealt me nothing but dirty deals since I was seven. I'd have to make it on my own, but next time I wouldn't get caught.

After my release from Yerba Buena, I headed for Bakersfield to see my mother. She was in pretty good shape, talking and making sense. She was still on wine, but the little children were away or in school, and she was managing alone. John had split, and Jackie was back in jail—caught stealing again. It was during this visit that Mama told me all she knew about the attack. She seemed relieved to discuss it, and neither of us asked, "Why was it Molly Tucker?" "Why were two little boys sent to Juvenile Hall where they learned to survive by becoming little crooks?" Life just was.

The would-be killer was now dead. According to a police officer, a man was killed at the Mexican border during a shoot-out over the smuggling of illegal aliens. Before he died, he confessed to the murder of a red-haired waitress in Los Angeles and gave her name. He never knew that she had survived.

Although Mama was friendly, she now seemed a casual acquaintance and somewhat restless around me. I had to move on—for her and for me. Just before leaving the next morning, I promised to reform. "And don't worry about me, Mama, just take care of yourself and the kids. I have friends and a job waiting." As I hugged her tiny frame, she promised to keep in touch. We each knew the other was lying.

It wouldn't make either of us feel better for me to visit Jackie on the inside, so I headed for Fresno. Lousy breaks. Everything about our lives was going to keep us separated permanently now. Standing with my suitcase in one hand and thumb out, I daydreamed for a moment about how it might have been if I'd had a dad like *The Man.* Then I began to walk briskly, disgusted with myself. *For cryin' out loud, don't start that again! He's a fairy tale. Grow up, jerk!*

Right then I held a mental funeral, vowing never to think of *The Man* again. He was dead, buried beside the road on the day I last saw my mother. As I walked along, hoping for a ride with each passing car, it seemed that I alone had survived. . . .

Chapter 13
THE BIG Q

Yeah, I'd survived all right. Survived to rob one more time, to get caught one more time. I stared through the cell bars to the dingy hall beyond, my mind forsaking its journey into the past for the realities of the present. Why had I let myself get talked into working with someone else on the dairy robbery? I always worked alone.

And by a girl at that!

Resolutely I got up off the drab-looking cot. Lying there examining the miseries of my life wasn't going to get me a better one. What would I do when they let me out of here? I'd heard of some operations going on in Hollywood. Maybe I'd fit in there!

Perhaps Arlene and the other women were right. Maybe I *was* capable of becoming a male model. Once on the outside again, I sent photos through an acquaintance to some "operations." If that didn't work, I'd hang around gay bars or somehow meet people with money. One thing for sure, I wasn't going to be poor—no matter what I had to do.

A male modeling job did open up, but about the same time I was caught in a burglary and sent to Lancaster for six months. Then I was transferred to Tracy, where I did eighteen months. Inside, my ability to impersonate various types of people made me the center of attraction and got me favors. In my twentieth year, acting the sissy role of a homosexual brought me drugs.

I'd graduated from sniffing glue and pill popping to shooting crystals and morphine, sniffing cocaine, or smoking the opium water pipe.

Having served my time, I again headed for Hollywood, older and wiser, and it paid off. I got the modeling job back, thinking the pay would let me stop my acts of crime.

At first I pulled enough jobs to get some decent clothes and supply my drug needs. I also connected in various gay hangouts. Soon I was able to get enough modeling assignments to provide a nice room and some money to live pretty good. I modeled swim trunks and things which showed my muscular physique. The hitch was, I was now supporting a drug habit of at least seventy to a hundred dollars a day. I pulled some jobs and connected in various gay hangouts to supplement my income.

One day an ex-con I'd seen in a bar approached with an appealing "business" proposition.

"Look what I got!" He displayed several cards from the International Detectives' Association. "We print these in the shop where I work. Whadaya think?" He grinned slyly.

"I think I just got us a good idea. You 'n me should become detectives."

Kicking around several ideas, we finally hit on a scheme to con local businesses into accepting our bargain protection service. Stealing enough equipment to appear legitimate, we dressed like proper detectives and walked into a business establishment. I flipped a badge and quickly tucked it into my pocket, then handed them the business card my friend had stolen. I told them we were with the International Detective Agency and working for a certain insurance company. We could cut their cost of coverage by twenty-five percent if they were interested.

Sure they were, so they listened. Of course, they could receive the lower rate only if they permitted us to examine their alarm system. This statement sometimes caused a raised eyebrow, so I hurried to add, "Please feel free to check us out with the L.A. Police Department." Luckily, no one ever phoned. We were shown various systems, deactivating certain areas and leaving them to appear normal.

The managers would be most helpful, even telling us where their hired guards were. We were smart enough to spread out the action, never taking enough at once to make it painfully obvious. Eventually we gave up this con game and sought other more exciting adventures.

Itchy feet soon led my friend, Joe, and me to El Paso, Texas, and into a tavern where the two of us sat side by side at the bar. A policeman walked in, came up to me and handed me a bottle. "Hit him," he ordered. When I looked puzzled, the officer explained, "We don't allow no darkies in here." A Puerto Rican, Joe was dark-skinned.

"But he's my brother," I objected.

Again the patrolman ordered me to hit Joe, so I took the bottle and smiled, "Thanks." Handing it to Joe, I said, "Hit 'em!"

Joe did, but another cop was watching from the patrol car. He rushed in and took us easily at gunpoint. We were driven to the local station and knocked around pretty good, so I popped a patrolman, too, before being placed in a cell. No one would believe that the officer had started it, so I wound up doing six months in the Texas workhouse for assaulting an officer of the law.

Luck deteriorated even faster when I returned to Los Angeles.

For pulling a robbery, I was sentenced to time at a California Youth Authority facility, where I promptly beat an inmate nearly to death with a rock because he made an improper advance toward me. At twenty-one, I was a ready candidate for San Quentin. I'd done a lot of illegal things, but none deserving of this place. Not the Big Q. Not Big Jim. One guy I knew who'd done time there called it Hell.

When I entered and the three heavy gates which immortalize maximum security prisons closed, I agreed. *Yeah, three gates to hell.*

I kept to myself during my two weeks in the Big Q. Even when I was transferred to Soledad I remained aloof. After a month or so, I was working in the shoe shop where I could sniff glue and was beginning to cope with life when a fight started. A guy had threatened to make me his sissy. I hit him first, which earned me solitary at Central Soledad.

Probably the cruelest treatment came from the jailer who handed me the telegram about Jackie's death, laughing tauntingly, "Ha, ha, Tucker, here's a letter at last." He knew what it said because the guards read our mail.

Jackie had died in Kern County Hospital a little after midnight on his twenty-first birthday. My grief was strong because I never got the chance to tell him that I was sorry after our last meeting and fight. Later I learned that he died of leukemia. Mama and one of my half-sisters were with him when he passed away.

My bitterness led me deeper into trouble, until I was sent back to the Big Q. There I incited a riot and was taken to solitary. From San Quentin, I went to Folsom and finally to a maximum security institution at Vacaville. There I was given fair treatment and, to my surprise, was paroled in about six months.

Back on the streets, big, hungry and scared, I was twenty-two. Loneliness and need drove me on a safe-cracking spree. Later joining forces with two men, I traveled from Los Angeles to San Francisco doing strong-arm and other kinds of robberies. We soon began working other states, and were about to rob the American Express Company office in Miami when we were taken into custody. I was extradited to California, which held more than six hundred counts of robbery in Orange County and Los Angeles alone. By the time the judge was through, I'd been sentenced to ninety years.

I arrived in Vacaville shackled and chained in a special car. Vacaville is the California institution where mental and incorrigible prisoners are sent for evaluation. I did my best to make the authorities believe that I was psycho, for then I could get placed on the medical side where I could get drugs and perhaps a cell alone.

I walked the halls talking to and answering myself. Also, I looked everywhere except where I should be looking, tore things up, and challenged guards to shoot me. It didn't work.

Next, I took a razor and shaved off the hair on every part of my body. I even gave a weird laugh, but nobody seemed to care. My antics only earned me a nickname: "The Animal." The psychiatrists weren't buying my act. My only break was a homosexual tag, which won me a cell alone.

Months later I was transferred to San Quentin, where I was involved in another fight and sent to Folsom. Still too young and fearful to go into the main yard, I kept alone as much as possible.

Before long I was back at Vacaville where some Christians tried to be my friend, inviting me to chapel. Because of Katie, I always respected the Bible, but could never forget my childhood experiences with so-called Christians. I never criticized those who wanted chapel to lean on, but it wasn't for me. In my mind the chaplains were just another type of guard.

Things went along pretty smoothly for a while when I began lifting weights. I enjoyed it and was still being given medication to keep me calm. When plans for a beauty contest were announced, I decided to enter. Always the impressionist, I took the title of "Big Jane," swinging my hips and flaunting my big frame. Using a mirror and lipstick as props, I swung along with a cheesecloth hanky and batted my eyelashes.

After I had won and things were back to normal, I was offered the chance to sell my body. I was big and tough enough to safely accept, extracting drugs, cigarettes, or anything else I needed from my victims. Pretending to be a homosexual was a racket to me.

In prison you never know when some incident may flare up that could cause you to lose life or limb. Even in sports the games are rough, played with everything you have just to let out hostility. Fighting is common during a game, especially in sports like football. As big as I am, I took my share in tender places, and dished out plenty, too.

I liked to be assigned kitchen duty. I still enjoy cooking, and it surprises some people that I am, and have long been, a gourmet chef. In prison kitchens I always did my best to find seasonings to make the food taste better. My job was to assist the hired cooks, who are out-prison kitchen supervisors. Most of them are okay, but now and then one will be a braggart. Those are the ones we tried to beat. It's like a game—steal food or foul them up so they'll become rattled or get in trouble with their superiors.

Once, while working in the kitchen and dining hall areas, some of the guys were goofing off by throwing a spoon or anything easy and close at hand at one another. One who had been to the library tossed a book into the huge tea urn. The red dye of the cover turned the tea red before we could fish it out.

With no time to make more tea, and to keep out of trouble, we just served it the way it was. To our amusement the tea was declared the best ever, and the inmates wanted more.

The tea incident may seem humorous in a pathetic sort of way, but in prison there's always a little something going on, and it makes some situations just a little bit easier to take.

We did some pretty rotten things to one another if we didn't like a situation. One time a guy was assigned to work with the kitchen crew who refused to take a bath. Among the milder things we called him was "Stinky," and it suited him. One day we commanded him to show up for work clean and smelling good. Although small-built, he was tough and refused. By force we tied him to the dish rack and sent him through the dishwasher. He was a mess when we finally let him out. One of the crew called a guard. "Hey, look man, this guy has really worked! He's sweatin' and he's sick. He overdid it. We're worried about him. Maybe he got overheated or somethin', so he'd better go to sick bay."

He was taken to the medical clinic but out of fear never talked. When Stinky returned to duty, he was clean and stayed that way.

Chapter 14

TURNING POINT

As my years in prison increased, I became harder. The nickname "The Animal" had stuck, for my mind was preoccupied with new ways to strike out at life.

There's no use going into detail about every rotten thing I did. It all happened, year by year, and is a matter of record. But never a day pased that fear didn't haunt my emotions. Yes, Big Jim Tucker had fears, the greatest of which was that I might never again be a free man. Any parole for me would be a long time coming. I'd be old when my turn for a hearing came, and older still if and when one was ever granted.

I learned to spend hours alone in a five by eight cell. The wire bed was hooked to a wall and had only a thin mattress to support my big frame. A small steel table was bolted to the wall; a seatless toilet and shelf were for my exclusive use. I was able to get a dresser scarf for the table and a rug for the floor.

At Soledad especially, I tried to stay alone because it's known as the gladiators' school. Fights with knives were almost routine. Prisoners there always found a way to have a knife, even if it was fashioned from a spoon or another metal object.

I was in all of the California prisons, but none improved my behavior. All attempts to straighten me out failed—group therapy, group counseling, community living, shock treatments, even the strip cell.

A strip cell is an eight by five concrete room with a steel door about two inches thick. There's another sheet of solid steel over the little window in the door through which food is passed. There is no toilet, only a six-inch hole in the corner with a steel rim around it level with the floor. The flushing mechanism is outside where only the guards can do it. The only light is tiny and of unbreakable glass, set into the ceiling. The cell has no bed or mattress and is soundproof.

Since I was considered dangerous and suicidal, guards took all my clothes, except my shorts. I remained there for three years feeling like a wild, lonely, caged animal with no hope of breaking free.

To give me thorazine, guards wearing heavy boots and dressed for battle marched into the room carrying a half-mattress. With that, I was pinned against the wall while the doctor gave me the shot. When the injections wore off and a guard opened the window to give me food, he had to be quick because of my violence.

During those three years, I was given at least three shock treatments. When they were finished, I was carried back and dumped onto the floor of the cell. This only increased my violence. The more they forced on me, the more my bitterness festered.

One day a compassionate new doctor came to the prison. He was shocked on his first visit to my cell.

"It's inhumane to subject this man to such treatment," he said disgustedly after the guards opened the steel door. "Mr. Tucker, would you like to get out of here? Guards! Get this man out!" he snapped. "Mr. Tucker, I'd like to help you. . . ."

The tone of his voice sounded convincing, and I believed him. At least he showed respect by calling me "Mr. Tucker."

Always the others had yelled something like, "Hey you," or "A-35689AB." I promised the doctor I'd try to stay out of the lockup.

I was immediately transferred from Vacaville to a newly constructed facility known as California Men's Colony East at San Luis Obispo, Las Padres.

At the colony I was permitted privileges long lost to me at Vacaville. It was good to associate again with the guys in the yard, to breathe fresh air and exercise freely.

CMC East was just another maximum security prison to me, a place to exist and survive. But, glad to be out of solitary, I wasn't about to look for trouble. I started to hang around with some black guys. They were great weightlifters, and I had a good outlet for my pent-up hostilities.

I used working out with them as another way to rebel against authority and get my own way. It meant nothing to me when some white Nazi gang inmates objected to my association with the Black Panthers. I wasn't interested in what they stood for, only that they had a great team.

It turned out to my advantage. There was something about those black men beyond their ability to do sports. They began to teach me how to apply basic psychology to everyday circumstances. I could see in Huey Newton, Jimmy Carr, Leon Huffman (not all were Black Panthers), and others in our group an admirable intelligence. And I admired their ability at self-control. These guys took a special interest in helping me, and I genuinely appreciated it. Often in tough situations I was encouraged by a soft voice, "Stay cool, man. You win by using your head, not your fists." By this, my black teammates taught me what the authorities hadn't been able to: don't place blame on those who are in control.

In time I was able to associate with guards and other inmates without getting into fights. At first it was an act, then wholehearted effort, to appear calm outwardly while seething inside. The team helped me to realize that it's normal to have emotions. The trick was to control them. Or at least consider the price you'd pay if you didn't. With practice I learned to master my temper without giving up the things I wanted, or giving in to anyone. It was a good feeling.

As usual I used this self-control to my own advantage. For three years, I ran protection rackets. The people I protected or "owned" paid me off in favors. Since no one sent me anything from the outside, those I protected shared theirs.

If there could be such a thing as a proud moment in prison, it was when I became one of the white guys of that time—1968 and 1969—to be among the top prisoner weightlifters in a nationwide competition. It was largely due to the encouragement of my black teammates. As a result of their influence in my first three years at the colony, my behavior record was pretty good. That, too, was to pay off for me.

When the parole system changed, I was called before the board for a hearing. By now I'd learned that nothing could be gained by wisecracks and decided to stand before the officers, smile, and say what they wanted to hear—"Yes, sir; no, sir."

"Frankly, Tucker, your record is bad—very bad—even considering the fact that you've not been in trouble lately," the spokesman for the board observed, scanning my file.

"Yes, sir."

"Your record shows that in all probability you'll be a habitual criminal; a change in your character or lifestyle isn't likely."

Right again, I thought.

"It is very serious to be classified as an habitual criminal," he continued. "Have you anything to say about this record? Feel free to discuss it. That's why we're here."

"No, sir, I have nothing to say."

Looking squarely into my face for reaction, he came to the real point. "The Habitual Criminal Act is now enforced strongly. If we let you on the streets again, do you realize that society would demand possibly the rest of your life in prison if further charges were proved against you?"

"Yes, sir, I understand."

"Well, Tucker, since you've got all that straight, there are a couple of things in your favor. You've never committed murder or rape, even though your temper outbursts began as a very young person."

The speaker paused again to study my face. I stood expressionless, waiting for him to continue. The man raised his eyebrows and kept his manner firm.

"Your sexual image in times past left something to be desired, too." He paused, and I just nodded my head.

The speaker glanced at the other members of the board, each nodding in turn as though casting a vote for an unspoken ruling.

"Tucker, we're going to give you one more chance to make it on the outside, and probably it will be your last. . . ."

I could hardly believe my ears and probably showed it on my face.

"Thank you, sir." Turning to leave, I remembered to look back and say, "Sirs."

"Wait a minute, Tucker. This parole has a condition."

Here it comes, I thought. Used to disappointments, I said only, "Yes, sir."

"You'll have to have a job and a place to go before you're released. Let us know when you find them."

There it was, the big hitch. "I will, sirs, and thank you again."

But who would give *me* a job? Who would let me stay with them, or find me a place to live? *Big deal! What a rotten way to give a guy his parole news,* I muttered quietly.

Yet this was one fight I had to win. I began to read the newpaper want ads faithfully and write to various places for a job. I wrote one hundred fifty letters applying for all sorts of positions, willing to do anything that would get me out. I wrote about the same thing to everyone, being honest about my record:

Dear Sir,

I would like to go to work for you. I've been incarcerated for twenty-seven years, and the longest I've ever been out since becoming an adult is six months at one time. I have only a sixth grade education and no job training. I am willing to work real hard as I need a job and a place to go in order to get the parole I've been granted.

Will you please help me?

Yours truly,
Jim Tucker

Each day at mail time I waited for a reply. Not one came. As the weeks crawled by, I wrote a few more letters, feeling jealous that others could leave because they had family, a place to go, some pull. My frustration and bitterness deepened with each mail call.

Some Christian guys had offered to help me when they learned I was applying for jobs, but I'd turned them down. I wanted nothing to do with those "Holy Joes." Observing my obvious failure, they continued to offer encouragement. "Don't give up, Tucker! There's a lot of good people out there. You'll hear."

"Yeah. Sure," I'd reply sarcastically.

My insides were churning because for the first time in many years I was caring. Caring that I had no family, that I had no true friends. Once I even let myself remember *The Man* who'd walked and talked with Mama. Why couldn't He be real?

Examining my life at age thirty-six, I resolved that if ever I got out and couldn't work and make it as an adult, the law would never take me alive. I often wondered what it would be like for someone to really care, to care about what happened to me, whether I lived or died.

As time continued to pass, it was apparent that the Holy Joes had singled me out for some kind of crusade. I admired their courage to stand up for what they believed, but I let them know that I wasn't about to listen to their preaching. Patiently, they continued to encourage me instead. Now and then I'd wonder what made them so happy, but figured it was because they had something in common within their own gang. I had my own way, I told them. "I worship freedom and power, and I'll do anything to get it!"

Good-naturedly they smiled at one another, as though sharing some secret.

"We're for you! You'll get it, Big Jim!" one grinned.

I shook my head. "You guys are fanatics. We're all in prison, and I don't see anyone around here who looks free to me."

In the library one day, one of the Holy Joes threw a book on the table near me. "Here, read this, Jim. It'll help you get out of here. The guy who wrote it knows all about freedom and power."

I picked it up and read the title, *Under Arrest!* by Phil Thatcher. Flipping it open, I spotted such words as "preacher" and "God" and "Jesus."

"Look, you guys, I got enough hangups. I know you like this sort of junk and you want to help me, but forget it. Here, I don't want to read no Christian book."

"But this is different. It's Phil Thatcher's own life story. He's the one who comes to speak to us in chapel. He's a right guy, and he said he'd help anyone who can get a parole and needs a place to go."

"No, man, no way! Don't you know? Christians only help other Christians. I've been in churches before, and when I get out of here it won't be because some Christian helped me."

They were ready for my answer. "We'll bet you twenty-five dollars in commissary that if you'll write to Phil, he'll answer."

I saw a cinch chance to win and took them up on it fast. "You've just got yourselves a bet—and you better have the goods when I win! And I ain't tellin' him I'm a Christian."

"That's okay. Write the letter any way you want to, just so it's the truth."

Writing the letter, I smiled wryly:

Dear Reverend Thatcher,

I have been incarcerated most of my life, but now I have a parole date of November 6, 1969. Some of the guys up here tell me that if you don't have anyone or anything out there that you will help them. But, first, I want to let you know (since I don't lie any more) that I am not a Christian, and I don't want to be a Christian. As a matter of fact, I don't even like Christians. Will you help me?

Jim Tucker

Finishing with the letter, I made out a commissary list totaling twenty-five dollars, confident that I'd win the bet.

Amazingly, Phil Thatcher did answer my letter.

Dear Jim,

Yes, we will help you. You're just the kind of hard-headed sucker we'd like to help.

Phil Thatcher

All I could say was "Wow!" Then, as if I'd read it wrong, I read it again—and again, wondering what he was like. I'd soon know, for a short time later he came to visit me, a first in my long and lonely years of adult imprisonment.

Incidentally, this was the first bet I ever was honest enough to pay off on. The Holy Joes got their twenty-five dollars in commissary goods.

Chapter 15
I FOUND THE MAN

Soon after receiving the letter from Phil, I was transferred to Chino Prison and told to await my release. Meanwhile, the chaplain had investigated me and was advised not to get involved.

The odds were ninety-nine to a hundred that I'd be into crime within thirty days. But Thatcher chose to ignore the warning.

Although I knew Phil would come, it still surprised me the day my name was called over the loud speaker. "Tucker, report to the visitors' area." It wasn't visiting hours, but he was a preacher and could come and go at his own convenience.

Thatcher is about five feet six or seven, and I was quickly looking down upon his partially-bald head, even as he stood. A man in his sixties, he stepped back and looked my tall, husky body up and down.

"You don't look so tough to me," he grinned.

It was a strange thing for him to say, especially to one with such a terrible sense of humor. In prison people smile while they knock your teeth out, but he was genuinely pleasant. I met his opening remark with silence.

"Well, I'm Phil Thatcher. Now, what can I do for you?"

As we shook hands, I blurted, "I need a job and a place to live."

He said,"Okay," then began to speak about the love of the Lord Jesus Christ and how He cared what happened to me.

"Hey, man, you didn't understand me," I interrupted. "I need a job and a place to go when I get out of here, that's all."

"Okay, you've got those. But I'm here because of the Lord, and He wants me to help you."

The chaplain talked a few more minutes about God, but I didn't try to understand, just tuned him out with my thoughts. *Some sort of phony business. He needs me for something, some racket. No one is going to help me out just for the fun of it—or even love, as he calls it. He just has to have an angle, but since I've got to get out of here, I'll play along with him.* Finally, Phil stood and extended his hand. "I'll be in touch, Jim."

He was true to his word. The day of my release came, and I was dressed out. The prison heads gave me someone else's outdated clothes, which didn't fit well, and thirty dollars. All the while, I was worried whether Phil would show up. What would happen to me if he didn't? But from the waiting room I spotted Phil sitting by the main gate. In a few minutes I was sliding into the front seat of his little old Rambler. Not much was said except hello. I sat as close to the passenger door as possible.

"Move over, Jim, and fasten your seat belt," he smiled.

"No, man, I'll sit right here."

"What's the matter?"

"Look, man, you're a preacher, an' I don't want you to preach to me all the way to Los Angeles."

He looked me up and down as he had before. "Well, if that's the way you want to go, man, go. If you want to go to hell, that's your business."

Never before had anyone talked so straight to me. In prison, on the streets, in bars, just about anyone I'd met—except

Katie—seemed to talk in circles. Especially in prison, where the need to survive was paramount over honesty. Phil's answer triggered a renewal of my fears. *Can I make it on the streets again? Does this preacher really care if I do?*

I couldn't understand Phil's frankness. Could I trust this preacher? He looked honest and pleasant, but I still wondered, *What's in this for him?*

I looked out the window and didn't move closer. *Imagine this guy. He's serious. Right from the guts, he tells me to go to hell. And he believes what he's saying.*

After a long while, Phil broke the silence. "Jim, I have to tell you something. If I was helping guys like you on my own, I wouldn't do it. Certainly wouldn't be messin' with you. But God gave me a love. A burden. And He gave me enough for you."

I glanced at him, then focused on the road ahead.

"You don't have to understand this now, Jim, but maybe some day you will. I just want you to understand why I'm sponsoring you. And from here on out I'm not going to preach to you. But just so you realize why I'm doing what I am doing—it isn't because of myself. I don't have what it takes to help you, but God does, and He gives it to me so that I can give it to you."

Phil had the straight, honest approach that I had looked for all of my life. He was right, no way could I understand what he told me. But I accepted it, believing that he did have something special from God. *If this guy doesn't turn on me, then he comes closest to The Man of whom my mother sang. So, he's all right in my book.*

Phil took me to a shabby but clean hotel in Lynwood near Los Angeles and paid for my room out of his own pocket. We shook hands, and as he was about to leave, he smiled, "By the way, Jim, how would you like to go out to dinner tonight?"

"Sure!" I was willing to take anything that was free. My thirty dollars wouldn't last long. Chuckling as he left, I thought, *Sucker!*

To my surprise that evening, he drove to the home of his friends, Mr. and Mrs. Leo Wagner in Torrance. Their hospitality was so relaxed and genuine that I could scarcely believe it. Did they know that I was an ex-con? If they did, it didn't seem to matter, for the smell of food was filling the air, and Leo's welcome handshake was firm in welcome.

"We're all set up and ready for you folks," Leo grinned, leading us to a table set for a king, buffet style.

"You first, Jim."

Filet mignon, baked potatoes with sour cream and chives, salad, homemade bread, pie and cake. I was ready for that steak dinner; it held my complete attention.

The others seemed more interested in talking than eating. They began with salad and coffee, relaxing and lingering over their food. Preferring hot food (in prison that is scarce), I dug right in. They didn't seem to notice my poor manners. I quickly polished off the first round, and looked at the three of them. "Better get some while it's still hot," I grinned.

"It's the Lord's food; have some more," Leo laughed. "Take all you want."

The others continued to nibble their salad and drink coffee while they talked to me and to each other. I heard them say something about, "The Lord supplies, and He's taking care of you, Jim. You're going to find out He is working for you."

Phil sat comfortably, smiling and enjoying their company, so I decided that if they were foolish enough to let me eat all their food, I would. I wolfed down three steaks, three potatoes and three salads, and topped everything off with a serving of each dessert.

Although I didn't understand these people, something in them caused me to respect their "philosophy," as I called it. Jesus, God, Lord and someone I'd never heard of before, the Holy Spirit, dominated their conversation. Yet nothing they said was pointed at me. As we prepared to leave that night, I thanked Leo and Agnes for the delicious meal.

"Wait just a minute, please," Leo requested, shaking my hand. He disappeared into another room for a moment, then returned with a black book in his hand. It looked vaguely familiar. Didn't Katie have one of these?

"I'm a Gideon chaplain, and I want you to have this as a gift," he grinned. "It tells you in this book about a Friend. He is a real Person, and He'll never cross you. He'll never snitch on you, and He'll never let you go. He'll be there with you as long as you want Him to be. He wants you to do right, Jim, but He'll be there even if you do wrong. This Friend will never do *you* wrong. He's also the kind of Person who'll forgive you when you do Him wrong.

"Jim, the time is going to come when you'll be lonely, when you'll even be thinking of something which could send you back to prison. When that time comes, look in the back of this book at the 'Sinner's Prayer.' Read it, and give this Guy a chance to be your Friend."

Having cleaned up all the food on his table, I felt obligated to take the Bible. "Sure, man. Thanks."

Once in my hotel room, I threw the book in the bottom dresser drawer and forgot it. As soon as Phil was out of sight, I caught a bus to downtown L.A., wondering if I could handle being on the streets again.

About one in the morning I called Phil. "Say, man, I'm downtown, and I'm sick . . . and I'm broke . . . and . . . I'm drunk. What're you doin'?"

"Trying to sleep, like all sensible people. Where are you?"

"Why, man, you gonna turn me in?" I wasn't supposed to be in a bar. I figured Phil would be like everybody else when he heard that I was drunk. But he wasn't. He came and picked me up, fed me coffee until I was sober, then took me back to the hotel. He was acting like that Friend Leo had said was in the book. He didn't snitch on me.

The next day Phil had a job for me. The truth was, I didn't want to work. Taking orders from anyone was not my desire. Besides, I had a pretty good thing going. Although the job was already mine, I walked out on the interview, telling the manager to forget the whole thing. I telephoned Phil and lied about being mistreated. Phil seemed to accept that.

"Well, we'll just find you something else."

I decided to play out the deal and see how long I could get away with it. He was paying the bills.

Before hanging up he said, "I'll be over to take you to lunch, Jim." This was another switch, and I couldn't figure it out. He took me to a private room in a restaurant, where a group of his friends had gathered. They belonged to an organization called Christian Business Men's Committee.

All the time we were eating, the fellows sitting with us hassled over who was going to pay for my food. Impressed, I decided to hang in with this bunch. *This is great. I've really got a good thing going,* I smiled to myself.

As we ate our dessert, a man told how God had changed his life. I didn't mind. He was an interesting speaker. *He's got a good thing going for him, too, even if it is God.*

Phil drove me back to the hotel and gave me some more money. Then as before I went out and got drunk. Again, I telephoned him in the early morning, and again he came to sober me up with coffee and take me back to the hotel. The same routine with Phil continued for several days—the luncheons, dinners, meeting Christian groups, free meals, good people—all the while I was unappreciative and growing more miserable.

One time Phil took me to a Full Gospel Business Men's Fellowship dinner meeting. What I heard was uplifting, even happy. Several fellows related what God had done for them and spoke of the "power of the Holy Spirit," as they called it. A main speaker gave a longer speech about a set of hardships that had been worked out by God, through His Holy Spirit.

Everyone in that room seemed happy, except me. Why wasn't I like those men? Probably this happy life was only for the lucky ones. They said that anyone could have it, but I didn't have it. I was too stubborn, anyway, to ever do what they called "surrender my will." I wanted to be my own man. This was fine for others. Not me.

December passed into January, and I was still doing my thing. Phil kept in touch, but I kept to myself a great deal, not wanting him to know I'd connected for some tranquilizers on the street. Phil couldn't have been kinder to me if he'd been my own father, and I didn't want to disappoint him.

It's easy for a guy on the skids to wallow in self-pity, and I did. Any reason would be an excuse for another drink, another tranquilizer, to lie in bed and not get a job. Sleep was nearly impossible, no matter what I took. Phil was leaving me alone, as he had others to look after. Plus he had a home and a lovely wife. Life was a waste, and boring. Lying on that bed in the hotel, I decided it was impossible to go straight. I wasn't about to go back to prison, either.

In that deeply depressed state, I considered pulling another robbery or finding some other way to get rich quick. It had to work this one last time. A real big haul so I could hit the road and get far, far away. No matter what happened, I'd not be taken alive.

As my plans formulated, I thought of the men I'd known outside prison. Most were either dead or inside. Only two were on the streets, and of those in prison, all were serving a life sentence.

Pacing the floor, I pondered crime opportunities one minute, death the next—not really wanting either. I just knew a change had to come in my life, and fast! The craving for excitement and money was overwhelming, but an inward desire to make it legitimately, and somehow live in peace, continued to nag at my conscience. Home, family, car, a good life. All these things were beckoning.

Robbery seemed to be the only way. But the face of that guy on the parole board, and his warning about life in prison, were haunting. For sure, I'd screw it up and get caught. I sat down on the bed and began to shake. *I'm too young to do all of that hard time and then die there. They'd just put me in the graveyard behind Folsom without even a marker. Life is rotten. Miserable!*

Casting robbery aside, I recalled the movies I'd watched on TV called *Rat Patrol*. Whole cities had been wiped out with one machine gun. Then, the one with the gun had gone out in a blaze of glory.

Why not get a gun and at least try it? But where? My thinking wasn't rational, but as the booze and pills wore off, I made jokes about myself in front of the mirror. *You're such a loser, with your luck, the gun would probably jam, and all you'd get is handcuffs and shackles, just like before.*

I went over and threw myself on the bed again, hoping to fall asleep and wake up with another idea. *Forget that TV stuff. If you want to commit suicide, do it the easy way. Find a high building and jump. You'll maybe make the last page of the papers, but the job on you will be done.*

I did just that. Finding a tall building, I rode the elevator up as high as it could go, then climbed the stairs to the top. From the roof, the wind teasing my face, blowing my hair, I didn't like what I saw below. In a moment of fear, I sat down against a wall to think things over. It felt quite cool up there as I considered my intention. *With your luck, Big Jim, you'd only goof it up. Probably you'd break both legs or something, and live; then they'd send you to the mental institution at Vacaville again.*

I couldn't risk jumping either. My mind wandered to Phil Thatcher. What a special guy. Why couldn't I live, really live, and be like him? I thought of his friends who wanted to be mine—Leo Wagner, Demos Shakarian, many others whom I'd heard speak. They were truthful men, and they'd said anyone could have a happy, fulfilled life. Did that mean me, too?

Man, it would sure be great to have what they've got, to be like them—especially Phil. I thought of what I'd cost him in time and money and of how patient he'd been all the way, keeping his word, never preaching to me, just living the way Christians seemed to live, without hangups. But could I change? *He* had, I remembered, and he'd been in prison.

For sure, something had changed Phil. He'd kept his life good and had stayed clean for more than thirty years. Straight all the way, just like he talked. A good wife who loved him, a good home and enough left over for guys like me. No doubt about it. He lived what he said all the way.

Why had I been so messed up? So many "whys" popped into my mind, but it was time to get off that roof. Jumping was out of the question.

I caught the bus back to the hotel, reflecting on what I'd

heard over and over again since meeting Phil. Every one of the men who'd told his life story had said there was absolutely no help for them until they invited Jesus into their hearts. Invite Him? Wasn't God supposed to be there? Everywhere? And weren't God and Jesus the same? I recalled them saying something about just beginning in faith. *Faith.* Did I have it? I wanted to.

In my hotel room I remembered what Leo had said that evening. He was right. I had what he foresaw—trouble, maybe the kind that would land me back in jail. I needed the Friend he had talked about, the One who stuck when things got tough. Opening the dresser drawer, I took out the Bible and thumbed the pages. It all made sense now.

Leo's words had been, "When that time comes, Jim, give this Friend a chance." If that book had the answer, I would now look for it. There just wasn't anything else to try. Inside the cover, right at the top, were the words, "God loves you."

Laying the book on the bed, I got down on my knees. How could He? There wasn't anything about me that He could love. *I* didn't even love me.

Tears welled and spilled down my cheeks. I had not cried since childhood. At that moment, tough Big Jim was melting. "God, if You can love a guy like me . . . please, help me. I want the Lord Jesus to come into my life and change it, just like He did for all the others."

Suddenly and strangely, I felt His presence. I stayed on my knees for a good while and talked to Him, just like Phil and Leo had said they did. What I prayed is between me and God, but I made no brags, no deals. I was straight with Him.

It was cleansing to unload and talk things over. Now I knew that *The Man* of whom Mama had sung was real. I had found Him. I'd longed to meet *The Man* for practically as long as I could remember. Now in that lonely hotel room He had come to walk with me, and to talk with me, and to tell me I am His own! That day He took me just as I was, hangups and all and, rising from my knees, I felt a sense of real belonging.

With the Bible on the bed beside me, I fell asleep feeling peaceful for the first time in my life.

Phil picked me up early the next morning. Opening the passenger door, I threw the Bible into the seat of his car and grinned. "Phil, on January 8, 1970, I found the Lord whom you call your Savior. Now I have Him, too! And I'm gonna live for Him."

Phil immediately prayed for me and shared my joy. "You have a new life now, Jim. A chance for a new beginning. Read the Bible every day and apply it to your life," he counseled, starting the car. "You'll make it because a lot of people have been praying for you a long time."

Driving along that morning, I continued to bubble with excitement. "Phil, I don't hate anyone any more, even that officer who caught me the last time I got sent to prison. I'm gonna find that cop and tell him about the love of Jesus!"

Phil glanced at me, grinning at my new exuberance. He was as happy as I over my transformation. Still, he cautioned me to "Wait awhile. Don't look for him right now. It'll all work out. Give God a chance to set the time."

Amazingly, I listened to him and didn't resent his advice. Not only had *The Man* replaced my hate with love, He had given me the desire to submit to others.

So many good things began to happen right away that it was hard to understand. Phil got me another job—the third since my parole—this time as a second cook at a convalescent hospital in Norwalk. The routine was similar to that of institutions I'd been in. My task was to help get out the meals for the patients and clean up. Being in excellent physical shape, I would get up early each morning and run most of the sixteen miles to the hospital, then change into my work clothes. For the first time in my life, I was putting forth the effort to do something for myself. Never before would have running and walking that distance entered my mind, but I was happy.

I would be so tired at the end of the day, however, that my Bible reading soon was neglected. Phil continued to take me to various Christian functions, but I let that fellowship become a substitute for church and Bible study, depending on what others said and did for my spiritual growth. In reality, I badly needed strong Christian ties, for I was about to make a serious mistake in judgment.

Chapter 16
THE TASTE OF TRIUMPH

It wasn't long until I felt drawn to a twenty-year-old nurse's aide who worked at the hospital. She was the first woman to interest me since my parole. Perhaps it was her big, bright eyes that turned me on. I started writing little notes to her. Others saw love's budding blossoms and played matchmaker. She responded with sweet notes of her own until I finally worked up enough courage to speak to her. My first words were, "Will you marry me?"

"Let's talk about it," she teased.

Believing that our mutual attraction was love, I ran to Phil with the news. I was thirty-six and had a lot of catching up to do on life. This is one of the hangups of guys fresh out of prison. They've lost a lot of years and want everything now—job, money, wife, family. I was soon to discover that it doesn't work that way.

"I'm in love. She's the most beautiful thing you ever laid eyes on, and I wanna marry her," I told Phil excitedly.

"Wait a minute, wait . . . a . . . minute! Slow down," he laughed. "Are you sure you're in love? Let a little time pass, Jim. Get things together more. This isn't love; it's just a passing attraction."

I wouldn't listen to him. Buying Royce a cheap ring on the

way, we took the bus that weekend to Las Vegas where a justice of the peace performed a brief wedding ceremony.

Wanting to be a good husband, I told her about my lonely years in prison, and that I still had to work out some of my old problems. Among other things, I explained that my reflexes were quick, a habit of many years of trying to survive among convicts.

"Royce, please don't jump behind me because I move fast, even if I'm just bumped. And don't ever slap me because I might forget and hurt you—even when you're only kidding around. Remember, I'm not used to it, and I'll react differently from what you'd expect. I don't know how to just play if someone wants to hit or wrestle just for the fun of it."

For some time she heeded my warning, and we were living happily in our rented apartment. One day, for no reason, Royce walked out of our bedroom and slapped my face hard. Without thinking, I knocked her across the room and was about to hit her again when she let out a loud scream.

Her cry brought me to my senses, and I realized that something precious had been lost.

"Why did you do that?" I trembled, helping her up.

"To test you," she cried. "I never did believe all that junk you told me about prison and your quick reflexes. I still don't. You never did all the things you said. And for sure I never believed you'd hit me."

Although I apologized, our relationship was strained after that. Self-doubt began to fill my mind like before. *Can I really master my temper? Where do I stand with God now? Am I going to blow it again? Maybe I'm not going to overcome my temper after all.*

Still, I couldn't give up. There had to be a way to overcome my temper.

Our marriage tension added to the problems of dealing straight on the outside of prison. Sins of crime weren't my problem any more, but living in the world among imperfect people, including myself, was tough.

One day I was offered a supervisory job at another hospital. It had more responsibilities and, to keep up a tough image, I would go to the bar at night and drink with some of the employees. Although I continued to attend church and put a tenth of my income in the collection plate, it was becoming obvious to Phil that my spiritual life was on the slide. Sensing that things weren't right, he began to encourage me to be more regular in reading the Bible. Looking on this as a sign of weakness, I'd agree to his face, then do my own thing.

Meanwhile, the problems between me and Royce seemed to mushroom. Although married for one year, we lived together only a few months. She'd often go to her parents' or girlfriend's home, and I never knew for sure where she'd be. We soon admitted that our love for each other was gone, then separated.

Throughout these early months of my Christian life, Phil was faithful to his promise and didn't preach to me. Still, he had a way of getting through. Sometimes he would put an arm around my shoulders with an encouraging word. Other times he would take me to meetings where people would tell things about their lives that he hoped would reach me.

I remember one time in particular. A guy was pacing back and forth, waving a medical journal excitedly. "What you see up here isn't what the doctors say," he boomed. "In this journal it says I can't walk. But today you see me before you—a walking miracle of God."

His testimony got to me. As most ex-cons, I was a hardhead. Illustrations in life of God's love and mercy—like the parables that Jesus told—did more for me than any sermon. Phil's approach was to teach by example.

The director of nurses at the hospital constantly complained about my work. Each time we'd get into it, I'd throw down my spat and threaten to quit. As usual Phil was there with a hand to lift me up.

"Jim, you're supposed to be living in love. You can't win anyone by walking out. You capture a swarm of bees by putting out honey. The next time she nags you, tell her how great she is. Find something good about her and see what a compliment will do."

When the director came storming into the kitchen one morning, I was ready.

"Jim Tucker! I want to talk to you!" she yelled.

"Miss Higgins, do you realize that you're beautiful?"

As usual, I kinda went overboard. She stopped dead in her tracks as I continued, "You've got the most lovely disposition of anybody I know. What is your favorite dish? I'd like to cook it—just for you."

The director glared at me in astonishment, then threw up her hands and stalked out. "What's the matter with you? Are you sick?"

In time my new approach turned our relationship around. But not without one last effort by her to goad me into another fight. Calling me into her office one afternoon, she handed me an ashtray. "Here, throw this at me," she demanded angrily.

"No, Ma'am. I refuse to fight with you any more."

"I want you back the way you were; you hear me, Jim Tucker? The way you were!"

"I'm not going back that way no more," I held firm.

This incident helped me realize that I didn't need to blow my cool. In helping me through circumstances like these, Phil made the principles of the Bible come to life.

In the Bible Jesus never went up to anyone and said, "Hey! Are you a Christian?" His actions made everyone want what He had. That's how Christ worked. And through Phil, that's what I've since learned to do.

I remember when Phil put his finger on the word "love" in the Bible the day of my parole.

"Jim, do you know what love is?"

"A four-letter word that has no meaning," I had sneered.

"No. God is love. "

"That's neat, man, but it's still in a book. What good's it gonna do me?" At that time, I had a problem that needed a solution. I wasn't interested in words from a book.

"We'll see," Phil had smiled.

And I did. Words can be cheap, but I was impressed with the way he put "love" into action. Like the morning we met a guy walking toward us just after we had left a restaurant. He wore stringy hair and filthy, ragged clothes hung sloppily on his skinny frame. Phil looked at his feet, covered only with tattered socks.

" What's the matter, guy, don't you have any shoes?" Phil smiled.

"No."

"Here, try these on." Phil reached down and took off his own shoes.

At first puzzled, the stranger slowly took the shoes. Slipping first one on, then the other, he grinned.

"Yeah, they fit."

"Good. Take them with you."

The guy started to leave, but Phil called him back. "Wait a minute. Did you eat this morning?"

"No."

"Go down to that restaurant and have some breakfast. Tell

the waitress that Phil Thatcher sent you."

Because of my drinking and poor relationship with Royce, life continued its downhill slide. Sometimes I wondered what was keeping me from the happiness that Phil and all of my Christian friends enjoyed. The missing link that had caused my marriage to fail was elusive. Yet Phil and his wife, Marie, had made it. And so had others. What was their secret? It was my search for answers that compelled me to attend church.

As I sat with other Christians, one of the greatest questions on my mind was, "Does God *still* want me?" Finally, through the Bible and my friends, I understood that God took me, sin and all, and would never let go. I had to face life's problems in God's power, not mine. Because He did actually live in me through the Holy Spirit, I could make it. This understanding gave me hope.

Royce came to me one day with the news that she was pregnant, wondering if we could get back together. Excited about the baby, I thought it would solve everything. We hugged, and I invited her back home. In the following months, we both tried our best to make the marriage work. I didn't ever want to lose my wife or child. Still carrying the scars from my own broken home, I wanted my baby to have both father and mother.

During free times from work, I took my Bible and sat in the park or wherever children passed. It seemed the Lord just drew them to me. I'd rap with them, about God mostly, but at times one would be encouraged to share a problem—something at home or school. Imagine me, a guy who had not had a decent home since age seven, and who had never done well in school, telling kids how to behave and warning of the consequences if they didn't!

Unfortunately, Royce had no interest in religion. We often went our separate ways, and that caused much loneliness. I tried to show her a good time in a worldly way, yet not let it affect my walk with Jesus. But it just didn't work. Walking the fence—on God's side one day and in the world the next—only added to my unhappiness. My double standard didn't encourage her to change.

Realizing this, I determined to get my life right again and live for the Lord. When Royce heard this, our communication troubles deepened. I did try to explain again my feelings about our lives together. But in vain.

"I've lived in turmoil and confusion all my life, Royce. I can't do that any more. You and I are one in God's sight. He intended for me to have a rich life in freedom . . . to be free inside as well as outside. I want to raise a family, not live in fear of you leaving me."

"You're a lousy ex-con, and a phony!" she screamed, cussing me out in words I no longer use. "Nobody can love you . . . you're an all-out loser, that's what you are! Won't never be nothing but!"

I continued to reason with Royce, begging her to pray with me and make our marriage work. She responded with more curses and threw things about the house. Storming into our bedroom, she tore at the expensive gowns and dresses I'd bought her and tossed them into the trash bin outside. Nothing I said could calm her. Finally, she bolted from the house and slammed the door behind her. Soon afterward she returned, begging forgiveness and seemingly resolved to make things work. She was like a different person.

Still feeling protective toward her and proud at becoming a father, I told everyone we'd worked out our differences. I blamed pregnancy for Royce's unpleasantness, telling her and myself that as soon as the baby was born she would be happy. I continued to hope that the baby would bring us even closer together.

I was thrilled when our son, Kyle Leon Tucker, was born. "He looks just beautiful, Royce. We're going to really be a happy family, a good family. It'll be a lot of fun helping you look after Kyle. I can hardly wait to get you both home from the hospital."

"Well, you can just forget it," she snipped. "I don't intend to go home . . . with you."

I was absolutely crushed. She left the hospital and went to stay with her friend. Now that our child had been born, she was determined to get a divorce.

Each time I visited Kyle my concern for his health grew. He suffered physically all the time with something. He was allergic to nearly all his food, and seemed to be a burden on Royce. After three months, she called me to pick up the baby.

"I've had him to the doctor again. He's not going to live. You can take him," she said sarcastically. "He has a disease that causes water on the brain and an enlarged head. You've been a failure all your life; you can't even have a normal kid! You deserve him."

I held my son close and tried not to believe it. Maybe she was wrong, or the doctors were mistaken. I'd have Kyle checked myself.

At Torrance General Hospital specialists were called in on his case, verifying what Royce had said. I refused to commit him to a special hospital for children as they advised, and took him home. If he couldn't live, I wanted him close, to hold him and watch him. I found a nurse with three teenage daughters who agreed to care for Kyle.

As the reality of the baby's illness set in, I began to blame

God. Why had He given me a son—the only person I'd ever had in my life that was mine—only to take him away from me? My anguish deepened as the weeks passed, and I called out to God just as a hurt child would cry to his father.

"Why, God? I know I've done wrong, but my baby hasn't. Why must he suffer? Are you punishing me for all my past? Why, God? Tell me why!"

The Man didn't answer. I realize now that I was suffering from a heavy burden of guilt.

I had always depended on Phil when trouble struck, and he was there then, too. "Your past isn't the problem this time," he counseled. "People may say they forgive when you do them wrong, but they never forget. Christ died for what you did, Jim. He already paid the price. When He forgave you, He put all that away; you don't have to carry that guilt around."

"Yes, but . . ."

"The Bible doesn't say 'Yes, but,' Jim. God gave His Son to save, not condemn. He isn't condemning you. You are."

Slowly I began to realize that, since God had come into my life, He had given me a new nature. Still, I couldn't shake my feelings of guilt. Inside, I wasn't right with God. It was hard to turn loose of my double life, to admit that drugs and the needle couldn't mix with my new nature.

"You've got a whole new life ahead of you, Jim. A whole new report card. What you do with it is up to you. You can't hide from God inside yourself—or your guilt. Step out and do what you know is right. Life's just like a baseball game. If you don't play by the rules, the umpire's got you out. Only, with God you've got a few more chances."

I had to like myself, Phil continued, because as a Christian I was important to God.

"He's been waiting for you to say, 'Yes, God, I'll go with You all the way,' " Phil smiled. "You didn't have to go through all that stuff in prison. God's freedom was open to you like a gift."

Phil's counsel helped my attitude, but it didn't make Kyle well.

"Have you tried praying for him?" Phil asked one day. "We've got hundreds of people praying for you and him. Why don't *you* try it?" His straightforward approach built up my faith and renewed hope. I prayed for Kyle from that time on, and was grateful to know of the many others who cared enough to stand with me.

One day during my Bible reading, I saw a verse which meant something special to me. "The things which are impossible with men are possible with God" (Luke 18:27). I thought about that verse in two ways.

First, about the thousands of dollars spent on me in prisons and institutions with no good results. Money had not helped me. Prison personnel had tried and failed. Only God could and did! I laid Kyle on the bed, then knelt beside him and began to pray. "God, he doesn't even belong to me. I see that now. He belongs to You. I don't even deserve him. I would love to keep him, but he's Yours. I give him to You right now, fully and completely. Do as You want to with him. I also give You my life completely, and I'll do whatever You want. I'll never turn against You again, and no matter what You decide about my son, I'll serve You with all of my body, soul and heart."

The next day Phil asked me to go with him to Camp Owens, where I had been sent as a little boy. He was to speak, but wanted me to explain where my life had taken me since my time there. I doubted that the kids would listen.

But Phil had a gift. Many of the boys did believe. To my great joy and amazement, thirty-eight out of a group of forty committed their lives to the Lord. Gazing at their sincere faces, I was speechless for several moments—deeply touched by the hope I saw for those boys, hope that meant they could make it. They'd never walk in my footsteps.

There at Camp Owens, a place I once hated with a passion, a new sense of direction filled my heart. I would point other kids to Jesus, even if they were already in a reform school or at Juvenile Hall.

From that time, I carried my Bible everywhere—living God's way and checking what I did by His Word. The presence of God was real in my life, and it kept me strong. I talked to *The Man* about everything, and He talked to me. It was just like the song said:

> *And the joys we share*
> *As we tarry there,*
> *None other has ever known.*

I had a real friend in Phil Thatcher, but in the Lord Jesus Christ I had found a Father.

Kyle was checked regularly at the hospital. As the doctors were reading his X-rays one day, they were startled. "Mr. Tucker, these X-rays have been checked and re-checked, and they show that Kyle's head is improving. We've done many tests, all of them carefully and thoroughly. His body seems to be catching up with his head size. Looks like he's going to live and get well."

With great rejoicing, I returned Kyle to his nurse, Virginia, and her three daughters, Rici, Beth and Robin. They had loved him as though he were theirs, and they rejoiced with me. In time he also was healed of badly inflamed ears and pronounced in almost perfect health.

The Lord Jesus wasn't through with me yet. When our divorce was final, the court gave me custody of our son—my son. Royce had a new life and didn't want to raise him. At the custody hearing, the police captain in Los Angeles appearing on my behalf called me one of the most rehabilitated ex-heavy drug users and ex-cons he'd seen in thirty years of police work.

Once more I had reason to thank God for His mercy and goodness toward me. Actually, He gave me my son three times. Once when he was born, once when he was healed, and once when I received permanent custody. I wondered how the Lord could ever give me more. Yet He did. Within three years, several people testified for me, and my parole time of forty-five years was canceled. As far as I know, I'm one of the first to receive discharges from three separate sentences, including violations of parole, burglary and grand theft, at the same time in the State of California.

When my parole officer brought me the discharges, he had tears in his eyes. So did I. Lawrence Means was an excellent officer, who with Phil Thatcher worked hard to help me adjust. This was a moment of victory for them, too.

The taste of triumph was good.

Chapter 17

LOVE'S TENDER BLOSSOM

Although Kyle was well, I still needed someone to care for him, and his nurse continued to do so—even adopting him and me into the family. As Kyle learned to talk, he called Virginia his mother.

My attachment to Virginia eventually flowered into love's tender blossom. She had taken great care of my son, arranging her schedule at the hospital to be with him when I couldn't and when her girls were in school. Kyle was now three, and I wanted us to have a real family of love. At just the right romantic moment, I proposed to Virginia and, to my great joy, she accepted.

She received the Lord into her heart one evening during a Full Gospel Business Men's Fellowship meeting. The people around the table were holding hands and praying. Those on each side of her raised their clasped hands in praise to the Lord, and she allowed hers to go up with theirs. Then the speaker gave an invitation to accept Christ as Savior. "Repeat this prayer after me," he said.

"Dear Lord Jesus . . . I believe You died on the cross for my sins . . . and rose from the dead that I might have eternal life. . . . I recognize my need of You . . . and I accept You now as my Savior and Lord. . . . Forgive me of my sins, and come into my heart. . . . Change my life, Lord . . . and give me the power to live for You. Amen."

At home that night she stayed awake, thinking of her prayer. No longer able to contain her exuberance, she punched and shook me awake. God had healed me of my quick, defensive reflexes, for Virginia had made me feel secure in our relationship. I sleepily asked her, "What's wrong, honey?"

"Jim, I really meant it when I prayed tonight. I took Jesus as my Savior. I'm a Christian now, too!"

For the first time in my life—after I married Virginia and she became strong in her faith—I knew what love really was in a family setting.

Once I suffered a crushed disk in my back and had surgery to remove it. Soon a second disk had to be removed. Lying in the hospital this time, I worried about my future.

"Lord, what if I can't use my legs? I'll be in prison again, only confined to a wheelchair instead of a cell. What woman would want me? I'm going to lose all the things I love as a family."

I was crying out to God in this manner when Virginia entered my room, took me by the hand, and began to wipe my forehead. Understanding my fear, she spoke softly and tenderly, "I took you for good or for worse, Jim Tucker. I don't care if you're in a wheelchair or what you are. I'm going to be with you and take care of you."

I still had back problems after leaving the hospital. Although able to walk today, I've been declared totally disabled. Right away, Virginia began working sixteen hours a day, while I devoted full time to the ministry.

She has been the backbone of my courage when things get tough and I'm tempted to quit. I remember one evening in particular. Having been used and mistreated by some guys that day, I flopped myself into a chair and fumed, "I quit!"

"No you don't! Go back and read your Bible and pray," she objected firmly.

"I don't have to put up with that kind of abuse, Virginia. Not me. Not any more!"

"If you quit, I'll . . . I'll divorce you," she stammered angrily. "You wouldn't be happy doing anything else." Her voice calmed. "'Sides, I couldn't stand you around here all the time—so go back and do what you're supposed to do."

Virginia is a dependable helpmeet not only at home, but in my ministry. Sometimes when things get hectic at the office, she'll take off work and straighten the situation out. Then she'll go back to her job. In time the ministry will grow to the point she can quit her nursing and be with me fulltime. Until then, she's content to minister behind the scenes. We truly enjoy what two people can become in the bond of God's love. We can communicate with each other and, if we don't want to talk, we can just touch and know we're one, that we're secure in each other.

God has given me the dream of my life. Phil, Virginia, her daughters, Kyle, five grandchildren. Sometimes our house is really jumping. But more than this, I'm welcome and loved as part of God's family. Everywhere I go, sometimes even in a restaurant or grocery store, someone will greet me with an enthusiastic smile. "Hi, Jim!" I like the feel of their arm around my shoulders. Being in God's family is the most important thing in my life.

Sometimes people ask Kyle, "Do you have a family?"

"Oh, yes," he grins and looks up at me. "We've got the largest family in the world, huh Dad?"

My lack of formal training has never been a big problem. Studying the Bible improved my education because it held so much practical knowledge about everyday life. One of my favorite Bible verses is ". . . all things work together for good to them that love God" (Romans 8:28). Although I've had my share of ups and downs, things *have* worked for my good.

Today I speak regularly in jails, prisons, and youth authority institutions, anywhere I can work with men and boys. In our office we have a twenty-four hour hotline, which enables me to extend God's love to many lonely and needy people all over the world. We also have a counseling and employment service for ex-cons. I'm often asked to go into Juvenile Hall to speak because if the kids are helped early, they seldom become repeaters. My friends among the police sometimes ask me to speak individually to youngsters and occasionally to their parents. Although my schooling is limited, God is using my past and the contrasting change in my life to reach men and boys behind bars with the message of hope.

Every opportunity I have for reaching them outside of prison is challenging and rewarding, too, for in this way they can be changed by Jesus before they suffer the embittering punishment that I endured.

Recently a teenager was caught running from a 7-Eleven store where he had stolen a bottle of wine. Instead of taking him to jail, the officers brought him to my headquarters.

"Jim, do you want him?" they asked.

"Yeah. I'll take him."

The youth was belligerent and tough as I ushered him into my office. "Brother, you could have gone to prison on a bottle of wine," I spoke firmly. "This isn't the first time you've stole things, is it? A bottle of wine isn't worth a year in county jail, man!'

For the next few minutes I told him about my life. "Now, I love you and care what happens to you. I'm going to let you go, but don't steal no more wine, okay?"

"Okay," he lied.

"By the way, what's that you got on your hip?" I nodded.

"A knife."

"What are you carrying that for? That can get you in trouble."

"I need it to whip those guys over in an apartment. I'm goin' to teach 'em a lesson they'll *never* forget!"

"Brother, you don't hafta fight people no more."

"Well . . . I gotta keep this so's I can keep in order."

"Before you could ever get to that thing, you'd be in trouble."

"Oh, yeah? If you're so tough," he challenged, "let's see you take it!"

As he reached back to unsnap the knife, I grabbed his arm and twisted it behind his back, running him head-on into the wall with a thud.

"See, I could have torn you apart! But because I love you, I'm going to let you go. I'd really appreciate it if you'd take that thing off, because I don't want to see you get hurt."

I put my arm around him. At first he pulled away. Then reluctantly he unfastened the holster and laid both it and the knife on my desk. I still have them in my possession, and the guy's involved in our Bible studies.

It's surprising sometimes how far a little love will go. I sent a Christmas card and package to a guy named Hercules once—just to show that I care. Today, he loves the Lord and is working with me in the ministry. This guy has twenty-one inch arms, a fifty-six inch chest, and a thirty-two inch waistline. He picks up tons of iron. Even tore a jail cell gate off at the hinges in county jail once. At forty-four, he's spent thirty-eight years behind bars. But now he's the meekest man I know. His whole life has been turned around because of what he saw Jesus do in my life. At this writing, he's at my office painting with a roller and brush—for free. We ex-cons never did anything for free before; now that's all we do. I don't get a salary for my work. Virginia provides our support, and the donations we receive go to help other prisoners.

It took awhile for me to mature in my Christian life. At times learning discipline and obedience was difficult. But perhaps my zeal got the best of me more often. I had something that was working in my life, something that was good for everybody. But I didn't have the wisdom to share it. When I'd see someone doing wrong, I'd tell them. Only they'd walk away ungrateful for my advice.

I didn't like that. One day I just reached out and picked up a fellow by the shoulders and held him in the air. Shaking him, I made my point. "Look, guy, you're a very fortunate man because God gave me love for you."

"What's . . . that . . . got to do . . . with things," he stammered, still suspended by my iron grip.

"Because God give me this love to display, and to give it to you. He loves you. But you don't want to pay attention, man. If I was my old self, I'd just set you down and beat the hell out of you!"

Later I found a better way to show love. You can't scare people into accepting Christ. When I set the guy down, he took off running. He'd have agreed to anything while I shook him in the air.

I don't have the education that most people enjoy, so in my speaking I'm just Jim Tucker. That's where God saved me; that's where He wants me. Just being myself and showing the love of Christ through my life is all that's necessary. Since my full commitment to the Lord, I've seen anywhere from one to five hundred receive Jesus every day.

I used to punch walls or people when things didn't go my way. Because of what Jesus did, today I'd rather put my arms around you and show that I care. Life is beautiful when you have Christ—even when things get tough. It's exciting to live because He makes it worth being alive.

It was the love of God, lived through a man, that did what no prison could accomplish. In the Bible Jesus declared that the gates of hell could not prevail against His followers (Matthew 16:18). It was into my hell that a servant of God—Phil Thatcher—marched, triumphantly shattering the bars of bitterness and hatred with the love of *The Man* of whom Mama had sung.

Prayer to Receive Christ

Dear Lord Jesus, I believe You died on the cross for my sins and rose from the dead that I might have eternal life. I recognize my need of You, and I accept You now as my Savior and Lord. Forgive me of my sins, and come into my heart. Change my life, Lord, and give me the power to live for You. Amen.

The Bible says that "If we confess our sins, he is faithful and just to forgive us our sins, and to cleanse us from all unrighteousness" (I John 1:9). If you said this prayer from your heart, Jesus has come into your life. You have just become a child of God.

Whether you are in prison or on the outside, I would like to help you. Just fill in your name and address on this page and send it to me. I'd like to pray for you and send you some helpful literature.

Jim Tucker
c/o Full Gospel Business Men's Fellowship
P.O. Box 5050
Costa Mesa, CA 92626

NAME ____

ADDRESS ____

CITY ____

STATE _______________________________ ZIP __________

Jim and Virginia Tucker form a prison ministry team. Virginia, a nurse, works as much as sixteen hours a day to make it possible for Jim to devote full-time to helping hundreds of prisoners to be released and make it on the outside.

Kyle Tucker is called "the miracle baby of Torrance Hospital." Kyle's serious birth injury and steadily declining health made doctors say that Jim Tucker's boy didn't have a chance. Prayers of Jim and friends changed that.

(Above) Parole Officer Larry Means, left, once told Jim Tucker: "I get nothing out of it if you go back into prison. My reward is in seeing that you stay out." (Right) An ex-convict himself, Phil Thatcher became Jim Tucker's sponsor so that he could be paroled. Phil and friends helped introduce Jim to Christ and revolutionize his life.